State

MW01595183

of Colleges and Universities

A Handbook for Institutions and Agencies

Second Edition

2020

Revised and updated from the first edition with additional material on case law, professional licensing, federal action and **SARA.**

Alan Contreras, Editor
Sharyl J. Thompson
Russell Poulin
Cheryl Dowd

A special publication of the State Authorization Network,
WICHE Cooperative for Educational Technologies,
In cooperation with *Oregon Review* Special Editions

ISBN 9798630687289

For Paul Shiffman, whose tireless work to improve access to distance education brought SARA to life when the conventional wisdom said it could not be done.

It could.

Contents

A note on references

Because the bulk of citations in this book are in material related to law and legal research, and two of the longer chapters were originally written in law review format, the citation form for most of the book is that used for law reviews, governed by the *Uniform System of Citation*, 19th Edition (Harvard) rather than the Chicago Manual of Style or another standard system.

Acknowledgements

Without the confidence and support of the people who hired me as a college program evaluator early in my career, neither this career nor this book would have happened. I must therefore thank the original risk-takers, Michael McManis and Robert Stein of the Missouri Coordinating Board for Higher Education staff who hired me in 1988, as well as Missouri Commissioners of Higher Education Shaila Aery, Judy Vickrey and the late Charles J. McClain.

Karen Garst at the Oregon Community College Association allowed me many years of experience with that sector, Ken Tollenaar, Jeff Luke, Sandy Arp and Kirk Bailey gave me the opportunity to work twice for the University of Oregon, and the Oregon Student Assistance Commission supported my work through twelve years of good times, miscellaneous legal actions and many successes in both Oregon and nationwide law improvements.

My predecessor David Young at the Oregon Office of Degree Authorization established and maintained genuine standards. For doing so he became one of the most disliked officials in state government—by those who did not have the strength of character to do likewise. To David, I say thank you, and bravo. I did my best to sustain that standard, as have my successors, Jennifer Diallo, Juan Baez-Arevalo and Sean Pollack.

Jesse Lohrke and Trimaine S. W. R. Belton, when students at the University of Oregon School of Law, and Jacek Berka, a 2016 graduate of the law school, assisted with research for the first edition of this book. Darcy Conners, a student at the University of Oregon School of Law, provided research assistance for the second edition. Stephanie Midkiff, Reference Librarian at the University of Oregon School of Law, was exceptionally generous with her time and patient with her customer. Carolyn Sinclair commented on portions of the manuscript and improved it greatly.

Michael Goldstein reviewed a portion of the text related to degree-granting authority and his comments were helpful in making it much better. Jennifer Diallo read much of the text and offered many useful thoughts regarding some of the ideas expressed herein. George Gollin, professor of physics at the University of Illinois, contributed a number of ideas.

Marshall Hill was willing to work with me at SARA 2013-2019 and we had a lot of fun while getting that new enterprise off the ground. Without Paul Shiffman's energy and vision there would be no SARA. I'm honored to be his friend.

Finally, the "new team" at SARA continues to work to make reciprocity as smooth as possible while retaining a commitment to the First Law of SARA: the right solution is the solution most beneficial to students. Working with Lori Williams, Mary Larson, Marianne Boeke, Jeannie Yockey-Fine and the rest of the SARA crew is always a great learning experience.

I hope that this contribution will be helpful to the many people at institutions, government agencies, the media and other entities interested in how degree authority works within and across state lines in the United States.

Alan Contreras
Eugene, Oregon
April 2020

Introduction

Why bother? Why do states and other regulatory agencies attempt to evaluate and oversee colleges? One view of the purpose and function of college degrees suggests that the government need not concern itself with whether a degree is issued by an accredited college or even a real college. This might be considered the classic libertarian view.

Should employers, clients and other interested people come to their own conclusions, based on their own research, regarding whether a credential called a "degree" is right for a particular job or need? This view is universally propounded by the owners of degree mills, who become wealthy by selling degrees to people who think they can get away with using them this way.

The libertarian view is tempting, but presupposes a capacity to evaluate that most employers have always lacked, while of course an average private citizen is even more removed from that ability and inclination. Who will actually do the research that the hypothetical perfect employer should do? No one.

Consider the complexities of the U.S. state authorization and accreditation systems, which even intelligent, educated people find opaque and confusing. Then add the proliferation of fake accreditors complete with names nearly identical to real ones (there were at least two fake DETCs, imitating the real Distance Education and Training Council, now the Distance Education Accrediting Commission, in the mid-2000s), phone numbers, carefully falsified lists of approved schools, web sites showing buildings far from where the owners have ever been and other accoutrements.

To the morass of bogus accreditors in the U.S., add the world. Hundreds of jurisdictions, mostly not English-speaking, issue a bewildering array of credentials under regimens not quite like American postsecondary education. Add a layer of corruption in some states and countries, a genial indifference in others, a nearly universal lack of enforcement capacity and you have an overwhelming quasi-academic slurry that even governments are hard-pressed to render into proper compartments. In one period of 10 days some years ago my office worked with national officials in England, Sweden, The Netherlands, Canada and Australia to sort out suspicious degree validations.

To this basic structure add constant change. Very few businesses and almost no private citizens are capable of doing the kind of research—the due diligence that an employer should require—without an exhausting allocation of time and resources. It does not and will not happen.

The alternative to some basic centralized determination of what constitutes a genuine, useful degree is a society in which any degree claim can be accepted or denied anywhere, any time, by anyone, for any reason. For this reason, governments have properly assumed responsibility for a certain level of evaluation and screening of degrees, and for overseeing at least part of what postsecondary education does. This book is about that activity, primarily at the level of U.S. states.

Basic concepts discussed in this book

The state of Oregon, where I was the chief college evaluator for twelve years, has the following statement in statute, which is a good starting point:

> **ORS 348.596** Purpose of ORS 348.594 to 348.615. It is the purpose of ORS 348.594 to 348.615 to provide for the protection of the citizens of Oregon and their post-secondary schools by ensuring the quality of higher education and preserving the integrity of an academic degree as a public credential.

Governmental functions often include the following components, not all of which are used by all jurisdictions.

1. Protection of citizens
2. Protection of post-secondary schools
3. Ensuring the quality of higher education
4. Preserving the integrity of degrees as credentials

5. Protection of colleges against unfair competition
6. Support for "bona fide" colleges
7. A basis for people to judge the competence of individuals
8. Enabling people to receive education commensurate with their talents and desires
9. Supporting training for economic or social reasons

These components are, in a nutshell, the reasons why society has established postsecondary regulation at all. Outside of academe and the most sophisticated large employers, few people understand the differences among kinds of degrees, types of accreditation and the different ways of determining the validity of degrees. For this reason, almost every state has at least some method in place through which people can obtain useful information about colleges. Also, every state requires at least some basic approval for colleges or minimal standards that colleges must meet to operate. These approval standards range from quite limited (distance-education oversight in New York and California) to very complex and detailed (e.g., Minnesota, Pennsylvania, Ohio).

One of the purposes of government control of degree-granting is to make sure that when someone is presented with a degree issued in the United States, it can be treated as a valid credential (absent forgery). Without that screening function, anyone could operate "colleges," issue "degrees" without any basis and operate as a pure degree mill. This, of course, does happen, but because it is done illegally, the "degrees" are always invalid. In fact, they are not degrees at all, which is discussed herein.

This handbook is divided into two sections. Part A includes mostly technical material on the legal mechanics of college oversight, particularly by state governments and agencies. Part B focuses on some specific issues that are of wide interest. My hope is that oversight agencies and college leaders will find it a useful way of looking at the academic enterprise. This second edition includes a new chapter on reciprocity and SARA as well as upgrading the existing chapters to bring them current regarding new legal actions and federal regulations.

In its entirety, the book is intended to provide some guidance to college evaluators and regulators of all kinds, whether they work for states, the federal government, accreditors or other entities that need to examine whether a particular college is an asset or a liability to society—or exists at all.

PART A – The Legal Basis for Degrees

Chapter 1

What is a degree?[1]

Alan L. Contreras

> "In practical affairs, [a degree] introduces its possessor to
> the confidence and patronage of the general public. Its
> legal character gives it a moral and material credit in the
> estimation of the world, and makes it thereby a valuable
> property right of great pecuniary value."

Supreme Court of Vermont in Townshend v. Gray

There have been many discussions among higher education
leaders in recent years regarding the problem of diploma mills and
suppliers of nonstandard or invalid educational documents.[2] One
key question that is often poorly answered is: what makes a real
degree genuine and a bogus degree false? There are many ways to
approach this question, but one baseline seems essential, that of
legality.

A clear line can be drawn between degree-granters that have
legal authority to grant degrees and those that do not. This is the
firmest rampart from which society can be victorious in the fight
against degree mills. My purpose in this chapter is to set forth the

---

1   An earlier version of this chapter appeared as *The Legal Basis of Degree-
     Granting Authority in the United States* and was issued by the State Higher
     Education Executive Officers in 2009.
2   See in particular GEORGE GOLLIN, EMILY LAWRENCE AND ALAN
     CONTRERAS, COMPLEXITIES IN LEGISLATIVE SUPPRESSION OF DIPLOMA
     MILLS at 21 STAN. L. & Pol'y REV. (2010).

current law that governs the authority to issue degrees in the U.S. This area of law has not had a careful collation of materials for many years, and I hope that this work will provide a useful baseline for discussions of the issues.[3]

It is important to note at the outset that the legal authority to issue degrees is not the same thing as the qualitative oversight of college programs, a much broader and more complex issue. It is also worth noting that a college having the legal authority to issue degrees is no guarantee that its degree programs are good or even adequate. One reason that the role of accrediting associations has increased in value over time is that some states have had poor or nonexistent authorization standards.

For an example of what can happen when a state fails to exercise adequate oversight of degree-granters, examine the entity that did business in Idaho, California and Wyoming under the name Kennedy-Western University and later changed its name to Warren National University when the kitchen got too hot. The published record of the Government Accountability Office and the resulting U.S. Senate and House hearings provide a window inside the world of state authorization when done badly.[4] The entity called Canyon College that operated in Idaho and California for many years is another example.

The question of how best to deal with degree mills in the labor market has been handled with admirable thoroughness by Dr. Creola Johnson in two law review articles,[5] and the overall problem of bogus degrees has been discussed in other recent articles and books[6] and is covered in some detail in Chapter 2. A

---

3   A very useful compendium of early cases is EDWARD C. ELLIOT & M. M. CHAMBERS, THE COLLEGES AND THE COURTS (1936). It is part of a series.

4   *Hearings Before the Committee on Governmental Affairs, United States Senate, 108th Congress, Second Session,* May 11-12, 2004. A companion set of House hearing transcripts is also available.

5   Creola Johnson, *Degrees of Deception: are consumers and employers being duped by online universities and diploma mills?* 32 JOURNAL OF COLLEGE AND UNIVERSITY LAW 411-490 (2006) and *Credentialism and the proliferation of fake degrees: the employer pretends to need a degree; the employee pretends to have one.* 23 HOFSTRA LABOR AND EMPLOYMENT LAW JOURNAL 269-343 (2006).

6   The degree mill problem is sometimes hard to describe to people who are not familiar with it. By far the best book on the subject of fake degrees

good recent overview of issues facing states in their oversight of for-profit colleges was issued in April 2012 by the American Association of State Colleges and Universities.[7]

The nature of degrees

In order to understand why certain credentials are not valid college degrees, and why some supposed degree-granters are called degree mills or diploma mills,[8] it is necessary to know what constitutes a *valid* degree. What this really means is that we need to know how a degree-granter obtains the formal authority to give someone a degree.

It is of some value to anyone interested in this subject to examine the historical origin of U.S. degree-granting colleges and

---

is ALLEN EZELL & JOHN BEAR, DEGREE MILLS (2005, second edition 2012). An excellent older reference with significant historical material is DAVID STEWART AND HENRY SPILLE, DIPLOMA MILLS: DEGREES OF FRAUD (ACE/MacMillan, 1988), which in turn refers to a useful 1963 dissertation later published by the Am. Council on Education as ROBERT REID, DEGREE MILLS IN THE UNITED STATES (University Microfilms, 1966).

The unique problems created by fake accreditors are set forth in ALLEN EZELL, ACCREDITATION MILLS (2007). This small book is not widely available and must be ordered directly from the Am. Assn. of Collegiate Registrars and Admissions Officers (AACRAO). A good technical guide to evaluation of degrees and transcripts called GUIDE TO BOGUS INSTITUTIONS AND DOCUMENTS has also been issued by AACRAO.

A useful commentary on the degree mill problem in Canada can be found in registrar Louis Ariano's 2004 conference paper downloadable from http://arucc2004.centennialcollege.ca /documents/A3.pdf.

7   Thomas L. Harnisch, *Changing Dynamics in State Oversight of For-Profit Colleges*, HIGHER EDUCATION POLICY BRIEF (SERIES), Am. Assn. of State Colleges and Universities, April, 2012.

8   The terms "diploma mill" and "degree mill" are often used interchangeably, but experts consider them to have different meanings: A diploma mill provides a fake educational document, but without any actual evidence or documentation, although it may bear the name of a genuine educational institution. A degree mill provides a degree with what purports to be documentation, but it is issued by a fake college. The term diploma mill is in more common usage and can be used as generic for both reptiles.

universities, therefore I have included some recommended sources in the notes.[9] The genuine colleges discussed in these historical overviews are many of the entities that today issue degrees in the U.S. However, pieces of paper that are called college degrees are also routinely sold by degree mills and diploma mills of various kinds, and can also be obtained from foreign countries.

A degree is a type of public credential, an *academic* credential.[10] A public credential is distinguished from other kinds of awards and recognitions in that it is used outside private life for a specific purpose. Legitimate degrees are given for certain accomplishments in fields of knowledge, within a structure that involves qualified teachers who evaluate student performance against a set of generally accepted norms. The institution then awards credit hours based on that student work (under the U.S. system, a system not used in many other nations), and when sufficient credits of the right kind are gathered by the student, that student is eligible for the award of a degree by the institution. Alternatives to the credit hour are discussed more often today and sometimes implemented.

Society has other kinds of public credentials, some of which are sometimes mistaken for degrees. The credentials most often confused with degrees are RN (Registered Nurse) and CPA (Certified Public Accountant), which represent an individual's

---

9   There are many excellent books on the subject of how U.S. colleges and universities came to be what they are today. Readers interested in the subject should certainly consider reading JOHN BRUBACHER & WILLIS RUDY, HIGHER EDUCATION IN TRANSITION (1958); LAWRENCE VEYSEY, THE EMERGENCE OF THE AMERICAN UNIVERSITY (1965); ROGER GEIGER, TO ADVANCE KNOWLEDGE: THE GROWTH OF AMERICAN RESEARCH UNIVERSITIES, 1900-1940 (1986, *rev'd* Transaction Publications, 2004); and THE AMERICAN COLLEGE IN THE NINETEENTH CENTURY (Roger Geiger, ed., 2000). More recent works covering the later 20th Century, such as GRAHAM & DIAMOND, THE RISE OF AMERICAN RESEARCH UNIVERSITIES (1997) and PHILIP ALTBACH, ROBERT BERDAHL & PATRICIA GUMPORT, AMERICAN HIGHER EDUCATION IN THE TWENTY-FIRST CENTURY (Second ed., 2005) are good collections of material on modern challenges.

10   The question of what constitutes an academic vs. "nonacademic" degree is addressed in CONTRERAS, COLLEGE AND STATE (2013).

certification, usually by a state licensing board, to practice as a professional. These are not degrees,[11] although the licensees usually hold degrees upon which the licensure is based, e.g., a associate or bachelor in these common fields. Some common ecclesiastical designations also carry letter-code designations, e.g., CSJ (Community of St. Joseph) or OSB (Order of St. Benedict). These are also public credentials used for group identification but are not degrees.[12]

One of the fallacies that even the best education researchers sometimes stumble over is the idea that we can expand the availability of educational offerings in the U.S. by allowing entities that are not colleges to issue credits or even degrees. For example, in one generally excellent study of the credit hour and alternate methods, the author notes the following:

> If we accept that college-level learning can occur outside of traditional institutions, then why shouldn't we accept that college-level credit could be granted outside of traditional institutions?[13]

We can't simply "accept" that any entity can issue college degrees or credit usable toward a degree. There is no private right to issue degrees, and many states regulate credit-granting, too. Certainly credits or degrees issued by an entity without proper legal authority could, at a minimum, be rejected by anyone. In many

---

11   The Court of Appeals of the District of Columbia mistakenly treated the designation "CPA" as a degree in the leading federal case on degree authority (Nat'l Assn. of Certified Public Accountants v. United States, 292 F. 668, 53 App. D.C. 391), but that error in dicta does not detract from the explanatory utility of the case.

12   One of the best overviews of the alphabet soup of degrees and related credentials is LEE PORTER, DEGREES FOR SALE (1972). This book, one of the earliest full-scale treatments of the degree mill problem, is also an excellent reference on what a real degree is and means, though in one chapter it mistakenly asserts that a charter as an educational entity automatically confers degree authority.

13   AMY LAITINEN, CRACKING THE CREDIT HOUR (NEW AMERICA FOUNDATION), p. 21 (2012). The full report may be downloaded from www.Newamerica.net.

states issuing such credentials is illegal; in at least one state it is a felony to issue degrees without a state license.

An entity that wants to be authorized to issue degrees has to demonstrate that it meets the standards for degree-granters established by a government. That said, nothing prevents an entity that currently lacks that authority from applying for it. A high-tech firm could certainly spin off a degree-granting unit, as long as it obtained the proper authorization.

Finally, an older but excellent detailed overview of the history and structure of genuine U.S. degrees, including reasons why U.S. degree labels have historically not matched up well with those in foreign countries, was issued by the Carnegie Commission on Education.[14]

Degree structures in Europe are now somewhat in flux, and degrees and credit structures that look more like those in the U.S. may become more common. At the same time, there is also some movement in the U.S. toward an evaluative system that does not rely on credit hours, but rather on a student's demonstrable knowledge and skills. This is gaining interest, in part because many adult learners are resistant to taking formal course work that trains them to do things they already know how to do.

The Council for Higher Education Accreditation (CHEA) offers a helpful, basic description on its website of what constitutes a degree.[15]

The basis of degree-granting authority

A degree is valid if it is *properly granted* (that is, not fraudulently or mistakenly granted) by an entity that has the *legal authority* to do so. There are three sources of authority to issue college degrees in or from the United States. A college can obtain that authority from **Congress**, a **state government**, or a recognized sovereign **Indian tribe**. Tribal authority is not quite the same as federal authority, because although only federally recognized tribes

---

14   STEPHEN H. SPURR, ACADEMIC DEGREE STRUCTURES: INNOVATIVE APPROACHES (1970).

15   *See* http://www.chea.org/pdf/Value_of_Degree.pdf.

operate colleges, once a tribe is recognized there is no apparent barrier to its chartering a college.

The three-source theory derives primarily from that part of the Tenth Amendment to the U.S. Constitution commonly referred to as the "Reserved Powers Clause,"[16] which recognizes that the federal government's powers are limited to those granted by the Constitution; all other powers remain with the States or the people. Education has historically been considered one of the most sacrosanct of these "reserved powers."

The states early acquired and have maintained a firm grip on education, about which the Constitution is entirely silent. States operate and control the bulk of the nation's K-12 schools and almost all of the public colleges. Except with regard to requirements wrapped around the provision of federal funds, Congress has (at least until relatively recently) generally avoided asserting significant direct authority in this area. That is why almost all of the law of postsecondary authority is state law, although many people forget that it is there.

The baseline that can therefore always be used to determine whether a U.S. entity is a genuine college or a degree mill is the answer to this question: which *government* authorized it to issue degrees? If it can't show that it is authorized to issue degrees by Congress, a state, or an Indian tribe, an entity purporting to offer a U.S. degree is a degree mill and its degrees may be treated as invalid (that is, not degrees at all), with possible exceptions for some degrees issued by religious schools exempt under state law, discussed in Chapter 3.

This chapter focuses on issues surrounding state authority to authorize colleges, as that is how almost all U.S. colleges obtain their authority. But first, a very brief look at the other two sources of authority.

---

16   The Tenth Amendment reads: "The powers not delegated to the United States by the Constitution, nor prohibited by it to the States, are reserved to the States respectively, or to the people."

Federal authority

Congress rarely establishes degree-granting institutions. Examples are the military service academies and a small number of related institutions such as the Community College of the Air Force. In addition, the federal government has a unique relationship to certain colleges operating in the District of Columbia, some of which it chartered.

A few colleges operated by the Department of the Interior Bureau of Indian Affairs are, technically, federally authorized, though they also operate with tribal authority and therefore might be called "hybrids" in the tripartite taxonomy of authorization.

Certain issues related to the federal presence in degree-authority cases are discussed below, where they fit more naturally into distinct subsets of oversight problems than they would in a discussion of the very small direct federal role in degree authorization. In general, federal authorization of degree-granting is not a significant factor in U.S. education.

However, it is important to note that some federal charters grant unusual kinds of authority. For example, Catholic University of America's original charter allows it to operate anywhere in the U.S., not just in the District of Columbia, provided that it has an agreement to do so with a local college.[17] These old charters are rarely referred to but can be quite useful in certain situations and should not be ignored.

Tribal authority

The right of federally recognized Indian tribes to charter degree-granting colleges without separate state authorization is widely accepted by state authorities. I have not reviewed case law on this issue because it is tangential to my purpose. There are a small number of colleges that are chartered by Indian tribes. The most well-known of these are schools such as Salish Kootenai

---

17   See *Laws Relating to the Catholic University of America* in EDWARD ELLIOTT AND M. M. CHAMBERS, CHARTERS AND BASIC LAWS OF SELECTED AMERICAN UNIVERSITIES AND COLLEGES (1934, Carnegie Foundation, reprinted 1970, Greenwood), p. 96, 100.

College (Flathead Nation) in Montana and Sinte Gleska University (Lakota Sioux Nation) in South Dakota.[18]

It is worth mentioning that tribal chartering authority does not convey accreditation any more than federal or state authority does. State laws requiring that certain degrees be granted by an accredited institution or program in order to be used (e.g., for professional licensure) are not affected by the original source of degree authority, as any college can choose whether or not to become accredited, and by what entity, whatever the source of its initial charter or authorization.

State action to authorize degree-granting institutions

By far the majority (over 98 percent) of U.S. degree-granting institutions, amounting to well over 4,000 colleges,[19] operate under the legal authority given them by state governments. State authorization is the normal method through which degree-granting colleges are established, although the nature of the legal basis for state degree-granting authority has rarely been discussed by courts or commentators. Broader understanding of the importance of state roles in this area is needed, as the recent lapse in this authority in California clearly demonstrates. The prominent if unusual example of California is examined in detail in the closing sections of this chapter, since it has significant implications for students, other states, and all of higher education.

---

18   There were 37 member and associate member colleges (plus one in Canada) of the American Indian Higher Education Consortium (AIHEC) as of March, 2020. For an excellent overview of how tribal colleges become established, see JOHN TIPPECONNIC, SUSAN FAIRCLOTH, CHERYL CRAZY BULL & GEORGE GIPP, A GUIDE TO ESTABLISHING A TRIBALLY CONTROLLED COLLEGE OR UNIVERSITY (2007, AIHEC, http://www.aihec.org/). For a good summary of the federal and tribal universe of approvals, see WILLIAM KAPLIN & BARBARA LEE, THE LAW OF HIGHER EDUCATION (Fourth Edition, 2006). Section 1.3.3 discusses federal and tribal authority.

19   About 4,100 accredited U.S. colleges are listed in the DIRECTORY OF HIGHER EDUCATION (2016).

State-conferred degree authorization appears in three basic forms:[20]

1. Public institutions owned or operated by the state or one of its subdivisions (such as a community college district),

2. Nonpublic institutions that have some kind of formal authorization to offer degrees, and

3. Schools formally exempt from some or all state authorization requirements on religious grounds.[21]

This chapter focuses on one aspect of degree-granter (nonpublic colleges) and one kind of state law and process (the process through which nonpublics obtain degree-granting authority) because this is the arena in which most of the issues surrounding degree mills and dubious degrees arise. It has also been the source of most litigation regarding degree-granting authority, and of much discussion in the unique legal situations that have caused problems in California and Texas, discussed below.

States claim to authorize nonpublic colleges to issue degrees in three ways:

1. Authorization by direct charter or some other kind of *sui generis* state action that approves specific schools *by name*. Many older charters were issued directly by legislative action or even, in their earliest form, by royal decree. There is some variation in how this was done, for example, some California charters were issued by the state's Supreme Court.

---

20 A good overview of the basic forms of state approval can be found in BRUCE CHALOUX, STATE OVERSIGHT OF THE PRIVATE AND PROPRIETARY SECTOR (1985). This publication was issued by the State Higher Education Executive Officers Association, but is now available only from the ERIC educational publication database.

21 Religious exemption is controversial, raises a variety of legal and policy issues, and is allowed in fewer than half of the states.

2. Authorization via a system of statutes and regulatory standards under which a regulatory agency grants authorization through a letter or formal license.

3. Authorization by *de facto* delegation of state authority to a religious body via state "religious exemption" statutes. See Chapter 3 for details of why this particular approach is flawed.

An excellent summary of key issues in the state regulatory environment, concentrating on technical requirements of each state, is set forth by Goldstein et al.[22] Another useful compilation which is intended to be updated on a regular basis (so far that has not been done effectively owing to lack of staff resources) is maintained by the State Higher Education Executive Officers (SHEEO) on its web site.[23]

Degree authorization by charter

Direct approval by charter or school-by-school legislative action is rare today, although there is no legal barrier (and some advantages) to it being done. However, it is the source of degree-granting authority of many older schools like Harvard, Dartmouth, and William and Mary. Even some relatively new institutions, particularly in the West, were established that way. Schools such as Willamette University (1842, still independent) and Western Oregon University (1856, now public) were established by charter issued by the territorial government prior

---

22 MICHAEL B. GOLDSTEIN, AARON D. LACEY AND NICHOLAS S. JANIGA, THE STATE OF STATE REGULATION OF CROSS-BORDER POSTSECONDARY EDUCATION: A SURVEY AND REPORT ON THE BASES FOR THE ASSERTION OF STATE AUTHORITY TO REGULATE DISTANCE LEARNING (2006). Dow, Lohnes; Washington, DC.

23 State authorization process survey information, some of which is out of date, is at: http://sheeo.org/sheeo_surveys/

to Oregon's statehood in 1859.[24] Whitman College in Washington was also established by territorial government charter (1882).[25]

The principal advantage (to a college) of having a charter is that it is usually permanent, barring exceptional malfeasance. Even if a charter is written to allow rescission, actually removing a charter granted by a legislature takes legislative action, which is typically slow and complex. Because charters are typically issued directly by a legislature, the college's authority is rooted at a high level in state government compared to having that authority based, say, in a letter issued by a low-level education agency or a license issued by an agency that doesn't even have education as its primary work.

The disadvantages are mainly to anyone who wants to call a college to task. Chartered colleges that do inappropriate things can be hard to bring within regulatory grasp, unless the action violates a separate law unrelated to the charter.

Authorization of this kind, based on historic norms (nine of the early grants of authority were royal charters issued prior to Independence) generally goes unnoticed and uninvestigated because of the nature of the schools: reputable, established, and nonprofit. It is precisely because these institutions have been around so long that no one looks carefully at their basic legal status; nor do many officials realize that the charter, that ancient and musty document, in fact has very significant legal consequences.

A good discussion of the importance of charters can be found in Clapp's *The College Charter*,[26] which sets forth the state of the law regarding the nature, importance, and limits of charters that give colleges degree-granting authority. It is noteworthy that the major cases discussed in Clapp's 1934 overview are still good authority today, as far as can be determined in a quiet backwater of education law.

---

24   CHARLES CAREY, GENERAL HISTORY OF OREGON (Third ed., 1971).

25   JAMES H. HITCHMAN, LIBERAL ARTS COLLEGES IN OREGON AND WASHINGTON 1842-1980 (1981). Occasional Paper No 17, Center for Pacific Northwest Studies, Western Washington University.

26   Gordon Clapp, *The College Charter,* JOURNAL OF HIGHER EDUCATION, 5:79-87 (1934).

Clapp notes that much law related to the rights of nonpublic colleges flows from the *Dartmouth College* case,[27] one of the few higher education cases that has remained among the Supreme Court's greatest hits. In this case the court concluded that the state could not rescind a charter given by the King of England to the college prior to the American revolution, because the charter was a contract and the constitution does not allow state action to impair contracts. A charter can contain provisions allowing for its rescission or change by a legislative grantor, but Dartmouth's lacked such provisions.

Some charters *do* include express legislative revision authority. Among these are the charters of Georgetown (a Congressional charter), Western Reserve University, NYU, Tufts and Northwestern. Indeed, some legislatures retained their authority to start with, even before the *Dartmouth* case; for example Connecticut's charter for Yale required the college "laws" to be laid before the state assembly "to be repealed or disallowed" as that body "shall think proper."[28]

The tangled early history of the chartered colleges is discussed in a number of books. A brief look at Harvard's early legal status gives an idea of collegiate establishment under unusual conditions:

> Although no mention of the power to grant academic degrees is to be found in the Harvard College charter of 1650, the institution conferred nine bachelor of arts degrees as early as 1642. This was a bold action; it amounted to an unauthorized assumption of sovereign powers.[29] ... Despite the cloud that hung over the legality of Harvard's charter, the college was able to carry on without interference until 1684, when the colonial charter of Massachusetts was revoked. With that revocation even any appearance of

---

27   Trustees of Dartmouth College v. Woodward, 17 U.S. (4 Wheat.) 518 (1819).

28   The Yale provision is discussed in L. W. Bartlett, *State Control of Private Higher Education*, p. 28. Teachers College, Columbia University Contribution No. 207, 1926.

29   John Brubacher & Willis Rudy, *Higher Education in Transition: An American History 1636-1956* (1958), p. 22.

legality for Harvard's incorporation vanished too. ... Consequently Harvard operated without a charter till 1707. In that year the Massachusetts legislature, standing on the thin ice that the charter of 1650 had never been formally repealed or annulled, directed the college authorities to regulate themselves from time to time according to the provisions of the original document.[30]

The issue of degree-granting authority has rarely been addressed by the courts; however, there are enough decisions to establish a solid and consistent baseline from which a discussion of this issue can proceed.

The leading federal case (indeed, almost the only federal case outside the Federal Trade Commission) is *Nat'l Assn. of Certified Public Accountants v. United States*, in which the Court of Appeals for the District of Columbia concluded that a corporation established under a general statute for educational purposes did not, solely by being so incorporated, acquire degree-granting authority.[31] The court held that degree-granting authority had to be granted in *express terms* by the government; in that case, Congress.[32]

The court, following a general principle expressed earlier by the U.S. Supreme Court,[33] expressly denied the association's "bootstrapping" claim that an educational corporation could give itself degree-granting authority by saying so in the documents of incorporation, noting the following principle consistent with previous and subsequent state cases:

---

30 Id. at 32.

31 53 App. D.C. 391, 292 F. 668 (1923), *cert den.* Oct. 6, 1923. Clapp erroneously called this a U.S. Supreme Court case.

32 This view was followed by the U.S. Department of Education in its interpretation of federal regulations in April, 2013, in which it concluded that a state charter as a nonprofit corporation was insufficient by itself to establish the authority to issue degrees.

33 The general principle that "bootstrapping" corporate powers through a bare declaration in corporate documents is not possible was enunciated by the Supreme Court in Oregon Railway & Navigation Co. v. Oregonian Railway Co., 130 U.S. 25, 9 Sup. Ct. 413, 32 L.Ed. 55 (1892).

Thus we see that, when Congress desired to give a corporation that power, it did so in express terms. From this it must be inferred that, where it did not expressly grant such power, it intended to withhold it ... when Congress thought it proper to vest a corporation with the right to confer degrees, it said so in express terms, and was not willing to leave the matter to conjecture.[34]

The U.S. Supreme Court decided not to hear an appeal from this decision, leaving the federal law of private-college degree-granting authority somewhat delicately poised. However, the court in the *Accountants* case was in effect following earlier decisions by state supreme courts, which serve to buttress the basic rule.

The Vermont Supreme Court in *Townshend v. Gray*[35] concluded that a corporation had no power to grant degrees under the state's corporation laws unless the legislature had expressly included that power in the charter. The court's impeccable statement of the situation is equally applicable today:

No express power to confer degrees can be found in the Statute under which this medical college was organized, and hence the power to confer degrees must be classed as incidental to the general powers of a corporation formed for the purpose of maintaining a literary or scientific institution, if it exists at all. ...

The power to confer degrees, not being conferred explicitly by the statute ... clearly does not exist at all. ...

Every state in the union has chartered these institutions, and it is believed that none of them has ever supposed that, with all the widely enumerated powers delegated to them, it had the power to confer degrees of any kind unless such power was expressly conferred in its charter. ... Such has, manifestly, been the legislative idea respecting the necessity

---

34   Accountants at 394.
35   62 Vt. 373, 19 A. 635 (1890).

of special authority from the lawmaking power of the government touching the right to confer degrees.

To hold that the Legislature, by a general law, intended that any three men in any town of the State, however illiterate or irresponsible, might organize and flood the state with doctors of medicine, doctors of law, doctors of divinity, masters of arts, civil engineers and all the other various titles that everywhere in the civilized world have signified high attainments and special equipment for professional work, is to liken it to the witty French minister who threatened to create so many dukes that it would be no honor to be one, and a burning disgrace not to be one.[36]

This case deserves to be viewed as the *de facto* leading state case on the subject (partly because the opinion is so clearly written), along with the rather turbid older *Medical College* case[37] below (from which the Vermont court shamelessly lifted the phrase about French dukes). The *Townshend* case was cited as recently as 1982 (see below under Religious Exemptions), for essentially the same principle, that degree-granting authority is held *in pectore* by state legislatures and must be granted explicitly.[38]

In the earlier *Medical College* case, not quite so clearly enunciated as *Townshend*, the Supreme Court of Pennsylvania also made clear that degree-granting authority must be expressly granted by the state legislature. It concluded that "... we look in vain for any such authority among the powers which shall belong to a corporation established under the provisions of this act, and if we do not find it there, we have not power to certify as to it..." [39] where the association's documentation confers powers not specified in the act.

---

36   Townshend at 636-637.

37   The Medical College of Philadelphia Case, 3 Whart. 445 (1838).

38   Although the term *in pectore* originates with Catholic practice, under which a pope can privately name a cardinal "in the breast" to be formally announced later, it seems an appropriate way to describe the special way in which a legislative body holds certain privileges (such as degree authority) closely, to be conferred in express ways as the body sees fit.

39   Medical College at 455.

In short, because the state's incorporation statute did not expressly include a right to issue degrees as a purpose for which an entity could incorporate, the court could not recognize such a right in the corporation that was asserting it in an application for incorporation as a college.

The court again clearly distinguished between such activities as literary and scientific work, which it considered reasonably within the powers of corporations, and degree-granting authority, which could be granted to a college only by *express* action of the state legislature. The Pennsylvania opinion is somewhat convoluted, and readers who venture into its murky corridors will understand why the Vermont opinion is held in higher regard.

Additional cases with essentially the same result in similar degree-authority conflicts can be found in the states of Maryland, Pennsylvania, and Massachusetts.[40] All of these cases conclude that degree-granting authority is legally separate from corporate existence or educational authority and requires an express legislative grant of power. A more recent opinion by the Pennsylvania Attorney General takes the same view.[41]

An alternate view by the Missouri Supreme Court in another very old case is something of an outlier, holding that degree-granting authority is implied when a college is brought into existence by formal state charter.[42] Elliot and Chambers in their book *Colleges and the Courts* commented dryly that the Vermont

---

40   Regents of University of Maryland v. Williams, 9 Gill and J. 365, 31 Am. D. 72 (1838); In re Duquesne College Charter (Com. Pl.) 12 Pa. Co. Ct. R. 491, 2 Pa. Dist. R. 555 (1891); Kerr v. Shurtleff, 218 Mass. 167, 105 N.E. 871 (1914).

41   Opinion of Attorney General Packel to John C. Pittenger, Pennsylvania Secetary of Education, issued Dec. 18, 1973, 63 Pa. D. & C.2d. 436, 1973 WL 41066, Pa. Dept. of Justice. The Attorney General made clear that degree-granting authority had to be explicit in law, and also embarked on a short informative history of the meaning of the words "diploma" and "degree" and how they had diverged in the past hundred years.

42   State ex rel. Granville v. Gregory, 83 Mo. 123, 53 Am. Rep. 565 (1884). In this case the college was established by express state charter that simply didn't mention degree-granting, rather than starting itself as a corporation.

21

decision in *Townshend* was "probably socially wiser."[43] Another commentator made the following very clear statement:

> The power to confer degrees is not one of the inherent powers of a corporation and, consequently, has to be expressly granted to institutions which wish to confer them. In the granting of this power the state has a definite means for exercising control.[44]

There does not seem to be any significant doubt about the limitations of the general-purpose incorporation process as a way to generate degree-granting authority: it cannot do so.

Degree authorization by state agency action

In addition to charters, there is the common, everyday process of state authorization[45] via an approval agency. Applying for state authorization and meeting state standards is the way that many U.S. colleges (especially those established in the past 75 years) obtained their authority to issue degrees. This is almost universally true for colleges operating outside their state of origin, but subsequent approvals of that kind are not of interest here because they always relate to schools that have already obtained their initial authorization. See Chapter 7 for more discussion of cross-border authorization. State processes have engendered a number of disputes over the years, perhaps most notably the *Nova University* case,[46] but because these have not produced many cases

---

43   COLLEGES AND THE COURTS, p. 203.

44   L. W. Bartlett, *State Control of Private Higher Education*, p. 49. Teachers College, Columbia University Contribution No. 207, 1926.

45   States use various terms such as licensure, authorization, approval and the like. Although these sometimes have slightly different meanings, I use the term *authorization* to encompass all formal state conferral of degree-granting authority by a non-charter process. This is the same term most commonly used by federal agencies and avoids confusion with terminology used by federally supported state agencies that decide which colleges are eligible for veterans funding; these are called "state approving agencies."

46   Nova University v. Board of Governors of the U. of N. Carolina, 267 S.E.2d. 596, (N.C. Ct. App 1980), *aff'd*, 287 S.E.2d. 872 (N.C. 1982). This

dealing with the ways that colleges obtain their *original* degree authority, they are not discussed in any detail herein.

Courts have in some cases[47] held that state laws were insufficiently specific in how they established standards for private degree-granters, but that problem relates more to the execution of such laws than to their conceptual basis.

A note on the Commerce Clause

Although the Commerce Clause in Article 1 Section 8 of the U.S. Constitution has not been a major factor in interstate degree cases, in one case a state's decision to treat its own colleges differently than those in other states resulted in an adverse ruling.[48] The case was appealed but the underlying statute was repealed in the interim and the case faded away.

Nonetheless, differential treatment remains a sleeping leopard in the regulatory forest. There is significant potential for an institution denied operational authority in a new state to take legal action on the theory that the state applies different (lower)

---

case also reaffirmed the states' basic authority over education. The Nova University case deals mainly with the issue of how one state can regulate activities of a college based in another state. However, the court decided the case in such a way that the result has some ancillary effect on our primary field of interest. Nova, an authorized Florida degree-granter, offered courses in North Carolina. The state objected on grounds that it had not granted Nova the authority to issue degrees in North Carolina. Nova responded by saying that the degrees were granted in Florida. The court held that because the right to teach and the right to issue degrees were not the same, a statute that regulated degree-granting did not reach so far as to allow the state to regulate teaching. However, when Nova challenged the District of Columbia statute, the college lost, primarily because the DC law applied equally to local and nonlocal providers. Nova University v. Educational Institution Licensure Commission, 483 A.2d 1172 (D.C. 1984).

47   Packer Collegiate Institute v. University of the State of New York, 81 N.E.2d. 80 (N.Y. 1948) noted a lack of sufficient standards and what subjects they should cover; State v. Williams, 117 S.E. 2d. 444 (N.C. 1960) dealt with similar issues.

48   Daghlian v. DeVry Univ., Inc., 582 F. Supp. 2d 1231, 1248–49 (C.D. Cal. 2008).

standards to its own institutions than to those based in another state.

Religious "exemptions" and degree-granting authority

Some states allow religious colleges to issue degrees without formal state authorization. This method of church-based degree-granting authority has expanded considerably, but with only the most nominal state attention. This has become a serious problem in degree evaluation and oversight of colleges. There are many so-called 'religious exempt' colleges around the U.S., but in every case the exemption is expressly established by the state legislature. This is therefore a hybrid system under which the state delegates its degree authorization powers to churches that want to start colleges that issue degrees. See Chapter 3 for a more detailed discussion of these issues.

Improper Claims of Authorization

An institution that operates in a state under one form or another of "exemption" or lack of state jurisdiction is not necessarily "authorized" there within the usual meaning of the term. Remember that authorization usually means a formal *authority to grant degrees* issued to a *named* institution. Exemption or ignorance of a category of institutions should not be treated as authorization.

That does not mean that an entity can't operate in a state at all. The question is not authority to operate as a business or authority to teach. The question here is the authority to issue a specific kind of public credential. However, exemptions and special status assignments of a similar nature are necessarily limited in validity to the jurisdiction that issued them.

Finally, keep in mind that the authority to teach, which is of special importance in cases of religious colleges and schools, does not necessarily carry with it the authority to charge fees for what is taught. This will vary state to state. In most states, charging a fee means that an educational entity is subject to at least some state consumer protection laws.

Delegation of government authority to accreditors

One of the fascinating changes in U.S. higher education over the past fifty years or so has been the emergence of entities called accrediting agencies or commissions, nominally private but *de facto* wielders of government authority.[49] Accreditors have existed longer than that, but their functions have changed over time. One of the reasons that the actual *law* of degree-granting authority has become so poorly recognized in recent decades is that it has been buried behind so many layers of accreditorial robes that many people forget that it is still there. The recent two-year implosion of California's college authorization process (see below) combined with renewed federal insistence on proper state authorization has blown away all but the flimsiest wisp of cover for this problem.

It is fairly common for people not familiar with U.S. higher education to assume that accrediting bodies are the sources of a college's legal authority to issue degrees. That is incorrect. While accreditation agencies are indeed relied upon by many governmental entities to perform certain qualitative, evaluative, or certification functions, they do not themselves have, and have never had, the direct power to *authorize* the existence of a college or a degree program. That said, the meltdown of an accrediting body can kill a college rather quickly, as we have seen as a consequence of federal recommendations to terminate recognition of ACICS in 2016.

---

49   See Lucien Capone III, A Guidebook to Due Process for Accreditors (2007), and his What, Me Worry? An Overview of Legal Concerns for Accreditors (2003), both prepared as conference papers for the Association of Specialized and Professional Accreditors and available from the association. For further discussion of qualitative oversight of colleges, there are many sources, but those of particular interest for their discussion of legal issues in accreditation include Sarah Molinero, Reexamining The Examiners: The Need for Increased Government Regulation of Accreditation in Higher Education, 51 Duq. L. Rev. 833 (2013)

Although accrediting agencies are well aware of the nature of their authority, this distinction causes more confusion than it should in state legislatures, and even within higher education. It is necessary to keep in mind that accrediting associations are membership-based and exist to serve the needs of their members. In many cases the information they gather from colleges is not even available to government agencies.

A state may conceivably delegate *qualitative oversight* of degree programs at a previously state-authorized private college (or indeed a public institution) to an accrediting body, although in accepting that role the accrediting body may find itself seen as acting as a quasi-governmental entity subject to certain legal norms. In some cases, private evaluative agencies such as accreditors or professional bodies may in fact provide better quality control than a state could, particularly if the state is lacking in higher education resources. However, states should take seriously their own responsibility for the quality of degrees issued under their authority.

I have seen no evidence that any state has ever delegated its power to *authorize* a college to issue degrees to a private accrediting body. Could a state do so? That is unclear, but it does seem clear that it could not be done without affecting the character of the accrediting agency. Such an agency that was delegated government powers might be treated as a state actor for legal purposes, creating expectations of due process and perhaps rendering the accreditor subject to public meetings and records requirements.[50]

In addition to serving the traditional role of qualitative oversight and ensurer of comparability, accreditors have been delegated, though the federal recognition process, certain gatekeeping functions related to college eligibility for financial aid and other programs. In that context, federal law states that

---

50   Degree authorization is not an innate power in accreditors, and they do not have mechanisms to do it, as they cannot issue charters or licenses and would need a formal grant of state authority to do so. It is not clear whether existing case law and federal rules, which set forth quite clearly the rule that degree-granting authority must be assigned by *express* state action, would limit a state's ability to delegate authorization authority.

colleges must have state approval *in addition to* and *prior to* accreditation.[51] State authorization is a completely separate and simultaneous requirement for student aid eligibility, and *current* authorization must be demonstrable at all times.[52] It is unclear what would happen if an accrediting body attempted to serve as the state authorizing agency as well as a federally recognized accreditor.

Federal recognition of state authorization

The U.S. Department of Education recognizes the states' primacy in determining degree-granting authority in the regulatory structure for eligibility for financial aid programs,[53] which provides the following definition:

> Legally authorized: The legal status granted to an institution through a charter, license, or other *written document* issued by the *appropriate agency* or official of the *State* in which the institution is physically located.[54] (Emphasis added.)

See the chapter on recent federal actions for more details. There is little case law related to the question of how the federal government reacts to or classifies state authorization requirements. One reason for this is that education is, absent congressional action, the province of the states. The bulk of

---

51   34 CFR 600.4(a)(3) requires state authorization; 34 CFR 600.4(a)(5)(i) requires accreditation or pre-accreditation. The CFR 600.5 series covers proprietary schools.

52   E-mails from Linda Burkhardt, U.S. Department of Education Region X, to author, December 5, 2007, reading "State approval and accrediting go hand in hand. Loss of either will result in a loss of institutional eligibility. ... State approval is one requirement and accreditation is another requirement. Both must be met at all times."

53   This area of law is constantly changing. See Chapter 6 for an overview of recent rulemaking trends.

54   Definitions are in 34 CFR 600.2. The state authorization requirement is at 34 CFR 600.4(a)(1). These in turn are rooted in 20 U.S.C. 1001(a)(2), which says that an educational institution must be "legally authorized within each state to provide a program of education beyond secondary education."

federal law (or at least federal money) related to the legal status of colleges flows from eligibility requirements for college students for federal financial aid such as Pell Grants or Stafford Loans.[55]

Federal law defining which colleges are eligible for student financial aid provides that in order for a college to be eligible for financial aid programs, it must be authorized by the state it is in. In addition, it must be accredited. The language quoted above would seem reasonably straightforward, yet in a previous and crucially different misinterpretation of the rules by the federal *Financial Aid Handbook*, this section of law was of some significance in a case impinging directly on the question of state authority over degree-granting.

In the *Sistema Universitario* case,[56] the Court of Appeals for the First Circuit concluded that for purposes of determining whether a college is eligible for federal aid, the U.S. Secretary of Education is allowed, perhaps even *required*, to determine whether a college in fact has appropriate *state* legal authority to operate in the state it is in, even when that state (in this case Puerto Rico, treated as a state for purposes of this statute) may take a different view. Puerto Rico's decision to recognize the college retroactively was disallowed (for purposes of Title IV eligibility) by the Secretary of Education.

The court's reasoning, which at first seems slightly out of true, is in fact rather carefully focused, and is based on the idea that because the Secretary is custodian of federal dollars, determinations of eligibility are necessarily in the Secretary's hands and can't become dependent on possible rogue approvals (or denials) by a state government. This is unobjectionable as far as it goes, but one of the legs that it stood on when it was decided in 2000 was faulty.

The court leaned with moderate weight on a specific provision in the federal *Financial Aid Handbook* in use at that time, which offered the following guidance to colleges in the 2000-2001 edition of the *Handbook*:

---

55   34 CFR 600.4, 600.5 and 600.6.
56   Sistema Universitario v. Riley (234 F3d. 772), 2000.

To qualify under any of the three institutional definitions, a school must be legally authorized by the state in which it offers an educational program to provide the program. The state's legal authorization may be provided by the licensing board or educational agency. In some cases, the school's charter is its legal authorization. *In other cases, a school is considered to be legally authorized if state law does not require it to have a license or other formal approval.* (Emphasis added.)

The last sentence, which was contrary to the plain language of the actual rule, was used by the court as a pivot-point from which the state's approval authority could be undermined in favor of the Secretary's ability to determine eligibility.

In 2003 the *Handbook* was revised,[57] and the revised language then read as follows:

To qualify as an eligible institution under any of the three institutional definitions, a school must be legally authorized by the state in which it offers an educational program to provide the program. The state's legal authorization is the legal status granted to a school through a charter, license, or other written document issued by an appropriate agency or official of the state in which the school is located. It may be provided by a licensing board or educational agency. In some cases, the school's charter is its legal authorization.[58]

The Department of Education intentionally removed the "silence is authorization" language, which was unsupported in the relevant Code of Federal Regulations (CFR), from the *Handbook*. A requirement that the authorization be in writing has been added, bringing the *Handbook* in line with the rule and with case law. Additional revisions occurred in 2011, and regulators should obtain current information. Current language in the *Handbook* is far more complex.

---

57   Changes to the *Handbook* can be tracked and compared using the U.S. Dept. of Education's Web site http://www.ifap.ed.gov/ifap/index.jsp.

58   The one-page section of the 2008-09 *Financial Aid Handbook* that explains the state authorization requirement is in Chapter 1, Institutional Eligibility, subsection 2-3.

The court did not make much of the disconnection between what is in the CFR and what was in the *Handbook*, but in fact the *Handbook*'s erroneous interpretive wording caused a misunderstanding of what the law really is. Ghost approvals of this kind (see the case study of California 2007-2009 below) appear unsupported by law.

For this reason, the *Sistema* case, although still a reasonable basis for the Secretary's authority over federal funds, is no longer of much consequence to the narrower matter of whether the Secretary has the ability to decide that a college has state authority for the issuance of degrees in the absence of a tangible, affirmative, state-issued document that says so.

It is extremely unlikely that even under the misinterpretation accepted by the court in the *Sistema* case, a determination made by the Secretary of Education regarding whether state approval of a given college did or did not exist would be binding in any way on a state. The decision carefully rooted that aspect of the ruling solely in the Secretary's responsibility for federal funds, and said nothing about state authority over colleges outside that context.

Federal rule changes related to eligibility for Title IV aid funds proposed in 2010,[59] adopted in part in 2011 and more or less settled in 2019 include express recognition that state approval cannot be conferred by silence, but must result from an affirmative act by a state entity that has the power to rescind approval and to act on complaints against approved colleges. This is a straightforward recognition of what case law says.

This rule, intended to preclude future problems of the kind that occurred in California, has created considerable discussion in states such as South Carolina, Wisconsin and Oregon, which have in effect grandfathered certain long-standing nonpublic colleges by exempting them from state oversight. The June, 2012 ruling overturning the federal rule by a federal appeals court on procedural rulemaking grounds has no effect on either case law or state laws.

---

59   See the U.S Department of Education's Notice of Proposed Rulemaking, Program Integrity Issues, 75 FR 34806-01 and the chapter on recent federal actions.

State Authorization and FTC rules

The Federal Trade Commission has been involved in the question of degree authority for some decades. FTC rules expressly place upon certain schools under its jurisdiction (for purposes of anti-fraud regulations) a requirement of state approval and makes clear that such approval must be expressly granted and cannot be inferred from a corporate charter.[60]

The principal FTC case dealing with state authority over degree authorization, which also touches on the meaning of "degree," is the *Cramwell Institute* case.[61] In this case the FTC found that it was a violation of federal trade law for a company to issue degrees without authority, and noted that:

> The evidence shows that degrees are lawfully conferred only by duly authorized, accredited and recognized educational institutions of higher learning as evidence of, and in recognition of, prescribed and substantially standardized scholastic attainments in various fields by students of said institutions. Unless such degrees are so well earned and conferred, they do not constitute degrees in the accepted meaning of said term and are of no meaning and effect whatever. A diploma is a mere paper evidence of the attainment of the degree. All of the evidence in this

---

60   16 CFR 254.1 - Definitions.
    (a) Accredited. A school or course has been evaluated and found to meet established criteria by an accrediting agency or association recognized for such purposes by the U.S. Department of Education.
    (b) Approved. A school or course has been recognized by a State or Federal agency as meeting educational standards or other related qualifications as prescribed by that agency for the school or course to which the term is applied. The term is not and should not be used interchangeably with accredited. The term approved is not justified by the mere grant of a corporate charter to operate or license to do business as a school and should not be used unless the represented approval has been affirmatively required or authorized by State or Federal law.

61   In the Matter of Joseph Jayko trading as Cramwell Institute, Etc. 55 FTC 242 (1958).

connection ... shows that the respondent has no authority
to award degrees or diplomas. ....

In the educational field, the words "diploma" and "degree"
have come to have a well-established meaning.[62]

The FTC has compiled a significant reference to its own older
degree mill cases[63] and continues to prosecute such cases today if
it has sufficient resources. Finally, the FTC maintains on its Web
site a degree mill warning page that provides good basic
information for people encountering a dubious degree supplier.[64]
See Chapters 2 and 3 for more information about degree mills.

*Recognition of state degree-granting authorization in Department of Veterans
Affairs rules*

Veterans benefits are available to certain veterans who attend
postsecondary institutions. Eligibility requires state authorization
of the educational provider, but also uses accreditation as a proxy
or a separate source of authority—or attempts to. The attempt
takes the form of a statement that if the state has no law through
which degree-granting is authorized, accreditation may be used as
a substitute. The attempt does not succeed.[65]

---

62   Cramwell at 269 and 279.
63   2 CCH Trade Regulation Reports §5083, pages 10,501-10,506 is a
      repository of older diploma mill cases.
64   The Federal Trade Commission site is *Avoid Fake-Degree Burns by
      Researching Academic Credentials.* http://www.ftc.gov/bcp/edu/pubs/
      business/resources/bus65.shtm.
65   Eligibility for veteran's educational benefits is governed by 38 CFR
      21.4200, which includes the following definitions:
      (h) Institution of higher learning. This term means:
      (1) A college, university, or similar institution, including a technical or
      business school, offering postsecondary level academic instruction that
      leads to an associate or higher degree if the school is empowered by the
      appropriate State education authority under State law to grant an
      associate or higher degree.
      (2) When there is no State law to authorize the granting of a degree, a
      school which:
      (i) Is accredited for degree programs by a recognized accrediting agency,
      or

We have seen that both state and federal courts require express grants of authority for *any* college to issue degrees; there is no such thing in the U.S. as a legitimate degree-granter that does not have governmental degree-granting authorization. Accreditation by itself cannot confer degree-granting authority.

(ii) Is a recognized candidate for accreditation as a degree-granting school by one of the national or regional accrediting associations and has been licensed or chartered by the appropriate State authority as a degree-granting institution.

(3) A hospital offering medical-dental internships or residencies approved in accordance with §21.4265(a) without regard to whether the hospital grants a post-secondary degree.

(4) An educational institution which:

(i) Is not located in a State,

(ii) Offers a course leading to a standard college degree or the equivalent, and

(iii) Is recognized as an institution of higher learning by the secretary of education (or comparable official) of the country in which the educational institution is located. (Authority: 38 U.S.C. 3452).

CASE STUDY

The Sacramento Quake of '07 and the repairs of '09

What happens to previously authorized or potential applicant colleges when a state allows its oversight and authorization of nonpublic degree-granting institutions to lapse, or abandons it altogether? This is a rare situation and has recently occurred only in California. California formerly had a statute that required some colleges to be licensed, and exempted certain other colleges from state approval requirements.[66] The legislature allowed it to expire on June 30, 2007, in view of the apparent weaknesses in the existing authority and the inability of the specialized state agency to use this authority effectively.[67] An excellent short history of the rolling blackout of California postsecondary education oversight can be found in a series of documents produced by the California Postsecondary Education Commission, itself a recent victim of state budget cuts.[68]

---

66   Codified as California Education Code, Title 5 Division 7.5, Private Postsecondary Education.

67   Having seen the former agency in action, I concur with this decision. For a front-row seat on the astonishing array of problems that the Bureau of Private Postsecondary faced and failed to solve, see BENJAMIN M. FRANK, INITIAL REPORT, CALIFORNIA DEPARTMENT OF CONSUMER AFFAIRS BUREAU FOR PRIVATE POSTSECONDARY AND VOCATIONAL EDUCATION OPERATIONS AND ADMINISTRATIVE MONITOR, Sep. 26, 2005, a 200-page tour of horrors. I am obliged to add, based on my personal knowledge of the situation, that some of the staff who worked at the former Bureau for Private Postsecondary were very competent professionals. However, the overall operational posture of the agency, its byzantine and ineffective funding methods, chronic understaffing and status as something of a pariah within state government made it almost unable to function.

68   The best starting point for an overview of the California situation is THE STATE'S RELIANCE ON NON-GOVERNMENTAL ACCREDITATION, PART TWO, produced by the California Postsecondary Education Commission (CPEC) in April, 1991. This clear, well-presented document provides both historical context and a modern political reality-check on oversight of private colleges in California, with recommendations for the future. There are other publications of that agency that are useful, including THE EFFECTIVENESS OF CALIFORNIA'S OVERSIGHT OF PRIVATE POSTSECONDARY AND VOCATIONAL EDUCATION (CPEC Report 95-13,

The state had no authorization laws at all regarding nonpublic higher education from July 1, 2007 through December, 2009. As a consequence, degree mills from the Tijuana River to Mt. Shasta argued that because it had no laws, no state approval was required to issue degrees and that anyone establishing a corporate existence can issue valid degrees. Degree mills such as Breyer State University, Canyon College, and Novus University relocated to California from Alabama, Idaho, and Mississippi, respectively, owing to the hole in the law. Even genuine accredited colleges make this spurious argument (as does a letter from the state's Secretary of Education[69]). This is the great risk of the "silence is authorization" position: Stanford and Novus end up in the same legal classification.

The previous law was dubious not only because of its history of poor enforcement but because it failed to recognize the state's duty to authorize degree-granting. It attempted to once again hand off *de facto* collegiate authorization of some institutions (i.e. those accredited by the Western Association of Schools and Colleges, WASC, a regional accreditor) to the accreditor itself. This offloading onto the Western Association[70] has long been known to be a bad idea. As one of the major explications of accreditation law put it,

---

October 1995) and an older, very detailed discussion, PUBLIC POLICY, ACCREDITATION AND STATE APPROVAL IN CALIFORNIA (CPEC Report 84-28, July 1984). An excellent historical overview of California law, including a facsimile of the 1850 act allowing the incorporation of colleges and information on how California law has changed over the years, is included in CPEC's PROTECTING THE INTEGRITY OF CALIFORNIA DEGREES (1989).

69   A letter from Glen W. Thomas, Secretary of Education of California, to the Oregon Office of Degree Authorization on March 24, 2009 includes the statement that in California "no approval is required to issue degrees." All available court decisions indicate that government approval is always required to issue degrees. Complete statutory silence regarding degree authorization appears to preclude the authorization of degree-granting colleges, *but see* the alternate view discussed in main text.

70   It should be noted that the Western Association's members have made clear that they want the Association, not the state, overseeing them. The Association staff works for the members and the members understandably want nothing to do with the problems that have plagued the Bureau for Private Postsecondary Education over the years.

Accrediting agencies' involvement in state licensure has further blurred the line between private accreditation and governmental action. Western has gone further than any of the other accrediting agencies by involving itself in state licensure. Under California's licensing statute, which Western actively supported, Western-accredited colleges and universities are exempt from the state licensure requirement. Moreover, the California licensing statute restricts the authority of state agencies to investigate complaints against Western-accredited colleges and universities. Western's involvement in state licensing caused COPA[71] to issue the following warning to Western:

> *In this situation, the accrediting body actively seeks to have its accreditation serve in lieu of licensure; if the accreditation is so used, there is a real possibility that the accrediting body will be found to be engaging in a state action (or at least a quasi-governmental action), namely, serving as an active participant in granting state licensure to an educational institution. Such a conclusion could result in imposing on the accrediting body the legal obligations imposed on a state agency, such as open meetings, [and] due process procedures . . . .* "[72]
(emphasis in original).

The California legislature attempted to fix this problem twice. In 2008 the legislature passed Senate Bill 823, but it was vetoed by the governor. In 2009 the legislature again acted with passage of Assembly Bill 48, which addressed some of these issues but did not confer degree authorization on any named schools. California's agency was technically re-established in early 2010, was operational by 2011 and finally named a director (fortunately a good one) in early 2012.

---

71   COPA was the Council on Postsecondary Accreditation, predecessor of the current Council on Higher Education Accreditation.

72   Michael W. Prairie and Lori A. Chamberlain, *Due Process in the Accreditation Context*, 21 JOURNAL OF COLLEGE AND UNIVERSITY LAW 61, at 67-68 (1994). This article is a superb overview of the issues in which accreditors can become tangled.

The Western Association, which recognizes that state approval necessarily precedes accreditation, expressed laudable willingness to work with the newly reconstituted Bureau of Private Postsecondary Education to create a mutually workable process for approving new private colleges that require or seek accreditation.[73] But it has taken too long—some colleges may have issued degrees that technically lack a valid legal basis. The legislation does not seem to recognize this and at some point the legislature may need to grant these institutions retroactive authorization to grant degrees, as was done in Nebraska when some of that state's nonpublic colleges were found to have murky authorization.

In California, the decisions and lack of decisions appear to work to the advantage of those private institutions that hold state charters antedating statutory requirements. These schools were, in effect, protected from competition by the state's 2007 policy decision, which appeared to disallow any new private colleges to operate in California (if we assume that California courts would follow the previous line of decisions requiring express authorization).

However tempting the "silence is consent" view is to colleges that find themselves devoid of any other option, it is unsupported in case law. The absence of degree authorization for a California nonpublic college lacking a charter that expressly authorizes it to grant degrees simply precluded it from issuing valid degrees between July 1, 2007 and the effective date of the 2009 law. Because such colleges have no inherent right as educational corporations to issue degrees, they need government authorization to do so. They existed *as educational institutions;* they simply lacked degree-granting authority. Of course, no such college stopped issuing degrees.

The contending theory that silence constitutes authorization is sometimes heard from California-based education offices. I do not believe that the concept is viable, as I advised the California Secretary of Education and several legislators.[74] There is simply

---

73 E-mail from Richard Winn, WASC, to the author, Sep. 28, 2009.
74 Several California colleges operate in Oregon, and the Oregon needed to have proof that they have degree-issuance powers in their home state.

no historical or legal basis for the idea that anyone may issue a degree without specific authorization from one of the three sources of potential authority. No U.S. court has ever recognized a private right of degree authority (that is, a personalized right to issue degrees flowing from the Ninth[75] or Tenth Amendment without government authorization), and that is all a business license or corporate filing consists of in this context.[76]

To sum up my argument, the authorization of degree-granting entities is inherently a governmental function in the U.S., as it is in almost all nations. Although a state may decide not to authorize any degree-granting colleges, if it wants to allow any to exist, it has to make an affirmative written act to name them.

There is an alternate view of the California situation. A noted higher education law expert considers my conclusions about California to place too much weight on the requirement that degree-granting authority be express and in writing. To simplify,

---

When it could not obtain this from the schools, it contacted Glen Thomas, California Secretary of Education, who informed Oregon that state authorization is not necessary to establish degree-granting powers in California. This is obviously incorrect (*but see* discussion of alternate views of how such approval can be provided), so Oregon sent a summary of the issues and cases to a number of California officials on April 4, 2009 (copy on file at Oregon Office of Degree Authorization).

75 For an interesting discussion of possible assertions of education-related rights under the Ninth Amendment, see pages 145-153 in DANIEL FARBER, RETAINED BY THE PEOPLE: THE "SILENT" NINTH AMENDMENT AND THE CONSTITUTIONAL RIGHTS AMERICANS DON'T KNOW THEY HAVE (2007). This is an excellent introduction to this sleeping giant of the Constitution. Farber only discusses rights related to K-12 education, but his guided tour of the largely empty but still living chambers of the Ninth Amendment is well worthwhile.

76 It is conceivable that someone unfamiliar with American law will argue that because every college has either a business license or is registered as a nonprofit, it has authority to issue degrees because its registry filing mentions education as one of its tasks. This argument, were the state to accept it contrary to the bulk of state and federal legal precedent, would result in the state taking the view that all degree mills and fake colleges are genuine and that their degrees must be accepted on the same basis. Many degree mills have business licenses or are incorporated. It would also follow that any business could issue degrees merely by adding "degree-granting" to its business purpose. The courts that have addressed this issue have not allowed this outcome.

his view is that the Tenth Amendment allows states to permit the establishment of degree-granting institutions via a silent statutory scheme (as then-California Secretary of Education Glen Thomas asserted) if a state so chooses, though he notes that such degrees may represent substandard or nonexistent student work and need not be recognized as valid degrees outside the authorizing state.

I contend, in contrast, that the entirety of court decisions requires an active statutory or charter system. This issue is very important not only with regard to the activities of genuine colleges, but to the prevention of degree mills and the proper classification of the bogus degrees that they issue. Under the "silence is authorization" view, entities selling degrees to all comers would have a legal status identical to that of legitimate private institutions. This outcome seems irrational as well as bad policy, and could lead to suits for equal recognition in employment or licensure of all degrees, those that are recognized and legitimate and others that are clearly bogus.

That said, the Tenth Amendment is a dimly lit structure that may prove to contain many surprises. Whichever view is correct, it is clear that degrees issued in such a vacuum need not be treated as valid outside the home state.

Conclusions and Recommendations

To be valid, a degree must be issued by an entity that has legal authority to do so. A college that operates without federal or tribal authorization to issue degrees must have degree-granting authority conferred upon it by a state government, whether by charter, express statutory authorization by school name or by written authorization issued by a state agency with statutory authority to do so. I know of no court decision holding that a completely silent statutory scheme means that any entity (indeed, any human) may issue degrees. While contending interpretations of existing law are possible, the facial absurdity of the probable outcome militates against alternative interpretations.

To avoid problems regarding potentially invalid degrees, degree-granting authority should, in the case of schools lacking a charter that expressly confers degree-granting powers for an indefinite period, remain in place at all times in the state's legal structure. Any states that have old or legally shaky statutory provisions for the authorization of degree-granting institutions should examine them with care to make sure that no schools are falling through the legal cracks, or could in the future. Nebraska, for one, has done this, a practical and laudable decision evidencing good leadership in that state, and other states should follow its lead.

Degree-granting authorization cannot be conferred by an accrediting body unless a state formally delegates that authority to the accreditor, in which case the state, to avoid Commerce Clause issues, should have a mechanism in place through which new degree-granters from other states can enter and operate even if they are not accredited by the local accrediting body.

Accreditors that are formally delegated state authority to confer degree-granting powers may become state actors subject to legal expectations of quasi-governmental or governmental bodies. Whether this is good (by causing decision-making by accrediting organizations, and the expectations and standards of such organizations, to be more transparent) or bad (by discouraging candor and placing negative accreditation reviews in the public view) is largely a policy question, not a legal one.

States that have religious exemptions for degree-granting institutions should adopt statutes that ensure that such degree suppliers actually have legitimate academic programs and are only allowed to issue degrees with religious titles. Chapter 3 provides a more detailed discussion on these issues.

Chapter 2

State action to eliminate diploma mill degrees

Alan L. Contreras

"Let us confess: The real object of education is the diploma. I never hesitate to declare that the diploma is the deadly enemy of culture. As diplomas have become more important in our lives (and their importance has done nothing but grow as a result of economic conditions), the less has education had any real effect. ... The aim of education being no longer the development of the mind but the acquisition of the diploma, the required minimum becomes the goal of study."[77]

— Paul Valéry

My purpose in this chapter is to set forth the current law, particularly state law, that governs the *use* of college degrees in the U.S. and to discuss what has changed in that law in recent years. This area of law has changed rapidly owing to the increase in the number of states regulating degree use and to the related attention being paid to the diploma mills that sell these degrees, both in the U.S. and elsewhere.

It is important to note at the outset that the ability to *use* a degree is not the same thing as the ability to *issue* a degree. The latter set of concerns, related to the legal constraints on issuing degrees, is discussed in Chapter 1.

Likewise, the question of the consequences of poor oversight of colleges and how to deal with bogus degrees in the labor market have been noted in Chapter 1 and publications referenced

---

77   PAUL VALÉRY, THE OUTLOOK FOR INTELLIGENCE (1962), p. 149. Bollingen Reprints (Princeton).

therein. The overall problem of bogus degrees has been discussed in other recent articles[78] and books, so I will not revisit that territory except insofar as it overlaps with the degree-use issues that are my concern herein.

Valid and invalid degrees

In order to understand why certain credentials are not valid college degrees, and why some degree-granters are called degree mills or diploma mills,[79] it is necessary to separate degrees from things that are called degrees but which are not genuine. This chapter focuses on those issues in the context of the degree user.

We often hear news media and even professionals in education and law enforcement talk about pieces of paper with words like "degree," "master of arts" or "PhD" printed on them as though there were some continuum along which degrees of many different provenances can be found. In fact, there is only one kind of degree issued in the U.S., and only one significant variation affecting U.S. degrees.

1. All U.S. degrees are issued by entities holding formal written authority to do so in the form of a charter, degree-granting license or similar explicit written authorization to issue degrees from a U.S. government at the state, federal or tribal level.

2. Some of the degrees issued under the authority of "1" above also hold accreditation from a federally recognized accreditor.

That's it. That is the entire universe of U.S. degrees (1) and the only really significant modifier affecting them (2).

So where do diploma mills fit into this universe? They don't. The question isn't what kind of degrees they issue, because pieces of paper that they issue are not degrees at all. They are simply pieces of paper with words printed on them. It is therefore inaccurate and confusing to refer to them as "diploma mill

---

78   See in particular GOLLIN ET AL., See Note 4
79   See Note 8 for the difference between "diploma mill" and "degree mill."

degrees" or even "nontraditional" or "online" degrees because in fact what they all are is simply *fake* degrees.

All degrees issued by U.S. entities lacking authority under (1) above are fake degrees. It is not necessary to evaluate them, compare them to real degrees or do any other kind of assessment of them. They are all fake all the time.

The term "unaccredited degree" is sometimes erroneously used as a synonym for diploma mill or degree mill degree. In fact, many unaccredited degrees are real degrees—about 20 percent of legally operating U.S. degree-granters, mostly small religious schools,[80] are not accredited. They don't have to be accredited as long as they hold proper authority to issue degrees from a government.

Accreditation is not a form of authorization, it is a certification of similarity to other schools in the private accrediting association. To put it another way, it says that each school that is a member of the association has met the group's standards, guidelines or norms. It is also used as a baseline proxy for eligibility for certain governmental benefits, such as student financial aid.

For an example of what can happen when officials misunderstand the nature of degree-granting authority, see the *Strang v. Satz* and Isom cases discussed below. Also review Chapter 3, on religious exemptions, and keep in mind that it is quite possible for a state-licensed degree-granter to issue genuine degrees that are of little or no value, for example the degrees issued by the late Kennedy-Western University under Wyoming law.

State regulation of degree use

Once degree mill paper is in use, what can be done about it? There are a number of ways that someone interested in eliminating bogus degrees can approach the issue. The fact that so-called "degrees" issued by unlicensed entities are inherently fraudulent

---

80 A survey of states conducted by the Oregon Office of Degree Authorization in 2008 resulted in the determination that about 20 percent of degree-granters in the U.S. are unaccredited. Most of these providers are religious colleges, but some are secular.

allows anyone presented with such a credential to decline to accept its validity without fear of legal consequences. An evaluator should always make sure to distinguish between *unauthorized* (always bogus) and *unaccredited* (status highly dependent on state law) providers. See the discussion of *Strang v. Satz* on the following pages for an example of what happens when the distinction is not well understood. There is more case law and commentary on this subject than on the basic question of degree authority.[81]

States often regulate the kinds of degrees that can be used for their own employees[82] or for purposes of state licensure to practice a profession. However, until recently it was relatively rare for states to regulate the kinds of degrees that were used in the private sector in professions that don't involve licensure.

The expansion of the degree mill business that accompanied the widespread availability of the Internet changed the way states think about degree use, mainly because of the sheer volume of fake and unaccredited degrees now pouring into the workforce. As of 2012, 13 states have some kind of law in place to protect citizens from the users of fake degrees.[83]

---

81   In particular, see Creola Johnson, Note 7 above, for an excellent look at the issue from a labor law and employer-based perspective. See also Joan Van Tol, *Detecting, deterring and punishing the use of fraudulent academic credentials: a play in two acts*, 30 SANTA CLARA LAW REVIEW 791-827 (1990), a case-based guide to what kinds of fakery actually happen. For a broad look at academic corruption issues, see Vincent Johnson, *Corruption in education: a global legal challenge*, 48 SANTA CLARA LAW REVIEW 1 (2008).

82   Oregon requires degrees issued by a college accredited by a federally recognized accreditor (or foreign equivalent), according to policy of the human resources unit of the Department of Administrative Services. Communication to the author by Beth Vergara, DAS Human Resources, Oct. 15, 2004.

83   North Dakota, N.D. CENT. CODE §§ 15-20.4-15 to -18; Maine, ME. REV. STAT. ANN. tit. 20-A, § 10802; Illinois, 720 ILL. COMP. STAT. ANN. 5/17-2.5; Indiana, IND. CODE ANN. § 24-5-0.5-12; Missouri, MO. ANN. STAT. § 173.754; Oregon, OR. REV. STAT. § 348.609; Texas, TEX. PENAL CODE ANN. § 32.52; Washington, WASH. REV. CODE ANN. § 9A.60.070; Nevada, NEV. REV. STAT. ANN. § 394.700; Virginia, VA. CODE ANN. §§ 23-276.1 to -276.12; South Dakota, S.D. CODIFIED LAWS § 13-1-52; Wisconsin, WIS. STAT. ANN. § 38.50, Florida, FLA. STAT. ANN. 817.567.

CASE STUDY:

Florida law and the misinterpretation of *Strang v. Satz*

Florida was one of the first states to attempt to prevent use of fake degrees, but owing to the wording of its statute[84], it was also one of the first states to lose a legal battle over the issue. The case is often cited as a reason why fake-degree laws can't be enforced. That view is based on a misunderstanding of the case.

In *Long v. State,* a Florida statute making it illegal to claim a false degree was upheld.[85] However, two years later the statute foundered—or appeared to founder—under the weight of a free speech argument in *Strang v. Satz,*[86] which made the crucial and appropriate distinction between accreditation and state authorization of a college. Government approval is mandatory for a degree-granting college to exist—there is no such thing as a legitimate unlicensed degree-granting college—but accreditation is optional. The state's decision to deny a degree-owner the right to say he held the degree was deemed an unconstitutional speech restriction.

A Florida prosecutor recently declined to pursue a case of falsely claiming a degree against police officers who were using fake degrees partly because he mistakenly thought *Strang* precluded the prosecution.[87] In fact, *Strang* only dealt with use of a *genuine* (albeit unaccredited) degree, while the police officers were using degrees that were *fake*, that is, they were sold by an entity (the so-called Almeda University) that did not have the legal authority to issue degrees in the U.S. at all. Using such a credential is no different than using one run off on a home laser printer.

The Florida statute made it illegal to use an unaccredited degree as a credential, and this wording created some confusion when people used the term "unaccredited" to mean the same as

---

84   Fla. Stat. Ann. 817.567.
85   Long v. State, 622 So.2d 536, Rev. Den. 629 So.2d 133.
86   Strang v. Satz, 884 F.Supp. 504.
87   Press release from Stephen B. Russell, 20th Judicial Circuit of Florida, August 11, 2006, accessed on the web on April 6, 2010.

"diploma mill." They are not the same. When the Florida federal court concluded in 1995 that the state's statute against the use of bogus credentials was in part unconstitutional, it concluded that because unaccredited Pacific Western University held a California license to issue degrees, users of those degrees could not be barred from stating that they held the credential.

The court decided the case correctly, so far as it went, but the afterlife of the case has shown a troubling lack of attention to detail by those who have subsequently engaged with these issues.

A brief digression into the nature of degree-granting authority as discussed in Chapter 1 may be helpful to an understanding of what *Strang* did and what it did not do. *Strang* dealt with someone using a college degree, and the court concluded that because the degree was issued by a licensed school, Florida could not make its use illegal.

What made the credential a degree? The fact that it was issued by an institution that had the legal authority to issue degrees. Because a credential *called* a degree that is acquired from an entity lacking degree-granting authority is *not* a degree, the label that it bears is irrelevant; it cannot be a degree if it is not issued by a valid authority. Any assertion that it is a degree or can be used as a degree is likewise baseless.

For this reason, it is not necessary to prove whether an online or mail-order provider of degrees is or is not providing an "educational experience" in order to decide whether its degrees are legally valid. It is only necessary to determine whether it holds valid authorization to issue degrees given by an acceptable government source.

Any degree claimant can be required to provide the name and address of the school from which the degree is claimed. A claim without that basic information can simply be ignored, as anyone can print a fake degree at home. If the name and address of the school is known, it is a simple matter to determine whether it has a charter or license to issue degrees from the jurisdiction it is in, and whether it issued a degree to the individual in question.

A claim that a U.S. school exists only in the ether, as it were, issuing degrees on its own authority without a formal government license to do so, can also be ignored. All such degree claims are inherently false and all such suppliers are degree mills.

The court in *Strang v. Satz* came to the following perfectly reasonable conclusion:

> Commercial speech must be truthful and must relate to lawful activity in order to receive protection under the First Amendment. The parties do not dispute the fact that the speech at issue is both truthful and concerns lawful activity. The speech is thus protected commercial speech.[88]

Readers of the case may read this language to mean that any claim of a degree from an unaccredited college is necessarily truthful and that all such claims carry a First Amendment protection. That is not a correct reading.

The entity from which Dr. Strang acquired his degree held a license to issue degrees from the State of California. That fact is what made Strang's degree claim truthful. Had his purported degree been from an entity such as "Redding University," which also claims to be located in California, the speech would not have been truthful because Redding University does not have a California license to issue degrees—it is a mail-order degree mill.

The same is true of entities such as "Youngsfield University," the Delaware corporation from which Florida police chief Mark Isom acquired a piece of paper called a degree, leading to considerable uproar in his community.

It is not possible for a degree claimant to *truthfully* state that he holds a *degree* from Redding or Youngsfield University. There is no such thing as a Redding or Youngsfield degree. The name "Youngsfield University" is simply a name, it is not a degree-granting institution.

The fact that a business registered its name as a "college" in Delaware is irrelevant. Delaware does not recognize its degrees and neither does anyone else. They can't. Because it has no license to issue degrees, its "degrees" are *per se* invalid and any claim of such degrees is by definition untruthful because they are not degrees.

---

88 Strang v. Satz, 884 F. Supp. 504, 508 (S.D. Fla. 1995).

The maxim that should be taken from these cases is this: **a degree claim can only be truthful if the credential was issued by an institution that has the legal authority to issue degrees.**

The fog of misunderstanding that has arisen around the Isom case is not unexpected, as so few lawyers have a working knowledge of how degree authority operates. In the St. Regis diploma mill case discussed by Gollin et al. (see Note 2), one of the defense counsel even wrote:

> There is no law or generally recognized definition of what does or does not constitute a "legitimate degree conferring institution."[89]

This is a remarkably ill-informed statement from a lawyer who had just spent a year or more working on the biggest degree-mill case in the U.S. in a decade.

There may well be good reasons why Fifth Judicial Circuit prosecutor Brad King chose not to pursue criminal sanctions against Isom, but his conclusion that it would be difficult to prove that Youngsfield was a degree mill is mistaken. It is very easy to prove whether a U.S. school is or is not a degree mill. If it is a U.S. provider, has appropriate licensure or a state charter and has no record of issuing fraudulent degrees, it is not a degree mill. If it lacks formal written authority to issue degrees, granted by a government, it is a degree mill and all of its degrees are fake. That's all a prosecutor needs to prove.

Isom needed to prove that Youngsfield had degree-granting authority under U.S. law. He can't. It doesn't. There is no such thing as Redding University or Youngsfield University or Almeda University in the United States. There is therefore no such thing as a U.S. Redding, Youngsfield or Almeda[90] degree.

---

89   *United States of America vs. Dixie Ellen Randock et al.*, Defendant's Joint Objections to Presentence Report, June 19, 2008, docket document 555. See 330 Fed.Appx. 628 (9th Cir. 2009) for more on the Randock case.

90   Almeda operated from Florida and from Idaho, but no degree issued from those states is valid owing to lack of state licensure. It later set up shop on the Caribbean island of Nevis. Most authorities do not accept college licensure by the pocket-nation of St. Kitts and Nevis (population

The Florida law remains on the books, but its utility is somewhat narrowed and it does not seem to be in active use. However, a prosecutor who used it in an appropriate case involving fake degrees should encounter no free speech issues.

45,000) because the country has no meaningful postsecondary oversight capacity and is a notorious home for degree mills. Therefore a "college license" from Nevis can be treated as having no more meaning than a generic business license. Almeda admitted in a recent case that under Michigan law its degrees are fraudulent. *City of Fraser v. Almeda Univ.*, 2016 Mich. App. LEXIS 82 (Mich. Ct. App. Jan. 14, 2016); see the case note discussion in Chapter 4. Classification of international degrees should be backed by at least one professional opinion from a reputable, experienced international evaluation firm.

Chapter 3

Do religious exemption laws result in an ungodly number of diploma mills?

Alan L. Contreras

One of the blurriest pieces of the U.S. degree-mill puzzle is the status of entities known as 'religious exempt' colleges that exist in 22 states.[91] In previous chapters we learned that a degree is valid if it is properly granted (that is, not fraudulently or mistakenly granted) by a college that has the authority to do so. What happens when the degree granter is a religious organization? States occasionally hear arguments to the effect that religious organizations have inherent authority to issue degrees under the Free Exercise clause of the First Amendment. That erroneous theory is discussed herein.

Can churches issue degrees?

States, which authorize over 98 percent of all U.S. colleges,[92] use two principal methods to authorize issuance of degrees: charters and licenses. Charters are generally issued directly by a legislature[93] while licenses, which take many forms and sometimes are simply a letter of authorization, are generally issued

---

91 As of 2012, religious exemptions are in effect in Arizona, Indiana, Iowa, New Mexico, Utah, California, Louisiana, North Carolina, Virginia, Florida, Maryland, Oregon, Washington, Georgia, Minnesota, Wisconsin, Hawaii, Missouri, South Dakota, Indiana, Montana and South Carolina. Most of these are "absolute" exemptions; Oregon's is a hybrid involving some statutory standards.

92 This figure is based on various sources and is arrived at by inference, since the number of colleges established by the federal government and Indian tribes is tiny, and there are about 4,100 accredited degree-granters in the U.S.

93 Some California charters, e.g. the charter for University of the Pacific, were issued by the California Supreme Court.

by a state agency empowered to do so. Religious colleges have obtained degree authorization through both methods.

Many colleges began under the administrative authority of churches or denominations. That is one of the traditional ways that colleges came to the U.S. and to the states—indeed, it is one of the prime original sources of college authorization.[94] However, one commentator notes that even early religious colleges "had to obtain special approval from the state before they could grant college degrees."[95] These early colleges trained people for the ministry, but did not necessarily grant degrees, and never granted degrees without a royal charter or one conferred by a government.

In the universe of religious life and leadership, degrees are mixed in with various kinds of credentials and formal badgings. Titles such as Father, Rabbi, Imam, Apostle, Deacon, Reverend, Ayatollah, Priest, Brother, Sister, and more obscure terms with specific meanings and functions (e.g., Oblate or Clerk[96]) abound. Many of these are used by teachers in educational settings. Some ecclesiastical designations carry letter-code designations resembling degrees, e.g. CSJ (Community of St. Joseph) or OSB (Order of St. Benedict). These are public credentials used for group identification but are not degrees. They are therefore not the concern of the government.

Most legal authorities agree that the issuance of degrees is a secular activity that is controlled by governments. There are a number of cases that deal specifically with this issue; one of the most often cited is the *Shelton College* case.[97] In that case, a religious college argued that because its beliefs precluded it from applying

---

94 An excellent look at the underpinnings of mainstream religious college authority from a Catholic perspective is Peter J. Harrington, *Civil and Canon Law Issues Affecting American Catholic Higher Education 1948-1998: an Overview and the ACCU Perspective.* 26 JOURNAL OF COLLEGE AND UNIVERSITY LAW 67 (1999).

95 Id. at 70.

96 An oblate is a lay person who affiliates in a formal way with a particular order such as the Benedictines. Clerk is the term most commonly used for the convenor of a Quaker silent meeting.

97 New Jersey State Board of Higher Education v. Board of Directors of Shelton College, 90 N.J. 470, 448 A.2d 988 (1982). It was really two cases decided 15 years apart, but the key case for degree authority is the 1982 case.

for state licensure as a degree-granting institution, it should be allowed to issue degrees because doing so was a protected function under the First Amendment. The court disagreed, concluding that

> … the State's program for licensing institutions of higher education is applicable to sectarian institutions and that facially it does not unduly interfere with the free exercise of religion nor create an excessive state entanglement with religion.[98]

Shelton College's defense was complicated by the fact that it issued degrees in several fields other than religion, e.g. English, education, business etc.

The Supreme Court of Tennessee reached a result similar to *Shelton*, with a cleaner set of facts that has the virtue of allowing the case to be viewed as the best national exemplar.[99] This case involved a challenge from Clarksville School of Theology, which only issued degrees in religious fields. The Tennessee court concluded that the issuance of degrees, even in religious subjects, was a matter for state control, because although the school's *educational* function was protected under a free exercise theory, the government has sole authority over all *degree-granting*.

In a similar case from Ohio involving a school that issued only religious degrees, the result was as in *Clarksville School*: degrees could not be issued without state authorization.[100] In that case, the trial judge found that the school could continue "teaching or offering to teach courses of instruction the content

---

98   Shelton College at 998. In Ill. Bible Colleges Ass'n v. Anderson, 2016 U.S. Dist. LEXIS 40496 (N.D. Ill. Mar. 28, 2016), Ill. Bible Colleges Ass'n v. Anderson, 870 F.3d 631 (7th Cir. 2017), *Shelton* is cited for the notion that providing for minimal educational standards in all schools is "a substantial state interest and secular purpose."

99   State ex rel. McLemore v. Clarksville School of Theology, 636 S.W.2d. 706, 5 Ed. Law Rep. 1294 (1982).

100   State Board of School and College Registration v. Ohio St. Matthew University of St. Matthew Church of God, Case No. 72-AP-130, Court of Appeals for Franklin County, Ohio (1972), unpublished, also cited by Nevada Atty. General Robert List in letter opinion cited in Note 106.

of which is wholly of a religious nature; provided, however, that no degrees or diplomas are issued, awarded or granted."[101] The Ohio appellate court found that

> While it is recognized that there is great merit, and a continuing need, for the teaching of theology and related religious subjects, it is also recognized that there is a great public need and necessity to establish a method of appropriate governmental review of those institutions offering professional degrees or diplomas as evidencing advancement by individuals engaged in the study of such subjects.[102]

The Attorneys General of Arkansas, Texas, Kentucky and Nevada have expressed similar views as to degrees; 'diploma' is generally considered a more generic unprotected term.[103] The Attorney General of Indiana concluded that the state could not regulate activities of religious colleges,[104] but the opinion did not indicate whether it was related to degree-granting schools or nondegree career schools. Also, it turned in part on the fact that Indiana law appears to ignore noncommercial schools, while forbidding state-approved schools from discriminating based on "creed," which the court found to include religious belief. For this reason, it is not particularly useful in the more common situation in which states *do* regulate nonprofits.

---

101 id. at 5.

102 id. at 10.

103 Arkansas Atty. Gen. letter opinion 2001-163, July 31, 2001, issued to State Sen. Ed Wilkinson; Op. Tex. Att'y Gen No. JC-0200 (2000), cited at 661 by the Texas Supreme Court in the HEB Ministries case but not reviewed in full for this book; 1988-91 Ky. Op. Atty. Gen 2-533, Ky. OAG 91-14, 1991 WL 53810 (Ky. A.G.), letter opinion of January 23, 1991 to Gary S. Cox, Executive Director, Kentucky Council on Higher Education; Nevada Atty. Gen. letter opinion by Robert List issued Sep. 7, 1973 to Merlin Anderson, Administrator, Commission on Postsecondary Institutional Authorization. The date on the Arkansas letter may be erroneous in the original.

104 Letter opinion (labeled "Official Opinion No. 22") from Atty. Gen. Theodore Sendak to Indiana State Senator Joan M. Gubbins, October 10, 1975.

The *Shelton College* and *Clarksville School* cases and their progeny are considered the leading cases and the logical result, but it is worth mentioning two cases that reached a different conclusion and have created turbidity in the legal waters.

The first of these is relatively minor. For many years, a Louisiana degree mill called LaSalle University sold degrees despite the state's efforts to close it. At one point, before the FBI finally acted to prosecute the owner, the school put a church on its property and asserted that it was exempt from state oversight under the state's religious exemption law. The state court agreed in an odd case related to the school's federal 501(c)(3) status.[105]

This relates to the problem of religious exemption in that it provides some support for the idea that anything that calls itself a church *is* a church. Whether this Louisiana theory, if used to support the issuance of degrees to all comers, would survive the *Smith* test[106] has not been established.

---

105 Ieyoub v. World Christian Church, 649 So.2d. 771, 94 0364 (La.App. 1 Cir 1994). In this case the Louisiana Court of Appeals held that the state had to accept at face value the school's statement that it was a 501(c)(3) tax-exempt organization and could not require the school to prove it. See also Rodrigue v. LaSalle University, 1997 WL 680575 (E.D. La., 1997, unpublished), in which a RICO claim against the degree mill was denied for technical reasons. LaSalle asserted a claim in meetings with state officials that even its degrees in chemistry and similar fields were protected as religious under Louisiana's religious exemption law because "all knowledge was divinely inspired" (letter from John Kay, retired chief of college approval for Louisiana, to the author). This is repeated in an inflated form in the first edition of Ezell and Bear's book on degree mills, which states that the Louisiana Supreme Court accepted this assertion. This is wrong. The only Louisiana appellate case relates to the tax status issue.

106 In Employment Division v. Smith, generally called "Smith I", 485 U.S. 660, 108 S. Ct. 1444, 99 L. Ed. 753 (1988) and "Smith II" 494 U.S. 872, 110 S.Ct. 1595, 108 L.Ed. 876 (1990), an Oregon law that imposed penalties on all users of peyote was upheld against a free exercise claim of use in a religious ceremony, and the court subsequently indicated that such decisions were properly legislative, not judicial, in nature. As of this writing, thirteen states criminalize or otherwise restrict the use of unaccredited degrees. The use of an unaccredited degree issued by a religious exempt school in Louisiana is therefore a criminal violation in some states under their general-purpose anti-degree-mill laws, which are

CASE STUDY:

HEB Ministries

The other church-degree outlier, the *HEB Ministries* case,[107] is far more significant and is based in part on a misunderstanding by a Texas Supreme Court plurality. In this case, the question was whether the state could require Tyndale Seminary, which lacked recognized accreditation or a state license to operate as a college, to obtain state approval prior to calling itself a seminary or issuing academic credentials. The case covered several issues including use of the term 'seminary,' state involvement in religious curricula, accreditation requirements and degree-granting authority. For purposes of this chapter only the degree authority issue is considered.

The District Court and the regional Court of Appeals backed the state's ability to control the issuance of degree credentials. The Texas Supreme Court reversed in a unanimous vote with eight justices voting and four varying dissents on the issue of degree-granting authority, which muddied the waters nicely.[108]

The court concluded that a seminary has a First Amendment right to issue religious credentials in religious fields without state oversight or approval. So far so good. It also got into a whirlpool over the meaning of "degree," which the court plurality, in order to reach the result it wanted, absurdly concluded that the seminary was not issuing.[109]

---

intended to protect the public from users of substandard credentials. It seems unlikely that any assertion of exemption can cross state lines.

107 HEB Ministries Inc. et al. v. Texas Higher Education Coordinating Board et al. 235 SW 3d 627, 226 Ed. Law Rep. 348, 50 Tex. Sup. Ct. J. 1094.

108 *HEB Ministries, Inc. v. Tex. Higher Educ. Coordinating Bd.*, 114 S.W.3d 617 (Tex. App. 2003). Justice Hecht and Justices O'Neill, Brister and Medina constituted the plurality that remained together on all issues; Justices Jefferson and Green dissented on the issue of degree-granting authority. Justices Wainwright and Johnson attempted to straddle the fence on the degree-granting issue by saying that the state could regulate the issuance of documents that had the word "degree" on them, but not the words associate, bachelor etc. Justice Willett did not participate in the case.

109 See Chapter 1 for a more detailed discussion of the degree-authority aspects of the case.

The seminary issued graduation documents using invented terms such as "Bachelor Level Diploma in Biblical Studies" as well as traditional Master of Arts and PhD diplomas that it baldly declared were not degrees.[110] In a technical sense, they are not degrees because the entity that issued them had no license to issue degrees, which means that in any other state they can simply be declared fake, but that was not the issue that the court looked at.

The court noted that Tyndale had never asserted that the state could not control use of the *term* "degree" and the majority rather casually concluded that "… HEB Ministries does not complain of the statute's restriction on the use of the word "degree", and we do not consider whether it is permissible."[111]

This makes no sense. The dissents, which take up half the opinion and are exceptionally well-researched (if sometimes opaquely written) on the matter of degree authority, somewhat neutralize the effect of the plurality decision. Indeed, in most respects the dissents coalesce toward the norm found in all other appellate cases of which I am aware. Justice Jefferson, for example, pointed out that

> … as Justice Wainwright notes, there is no doubt that the State is free to regulate postsecondary education, and thus may regulate the issuance of degrees (and degree-like documents) even by those who are religiously impelled to issue them.[112]

Justice Wainwright concluded that the case needed to be viewed in terms of commercial conduct, and acknowledged that the state had some power to control degree-granting, saying that

> … a contrary conclusion would allow entities, regardless of their motives, to circumvent the statutory requirements under the guise of religious practices by issuing degrees

---

110   The Coordinating Board correctly argued that the words associate, bachelor, master and doctor were inherently degree claims or awards when used in an educational setting; the court plurality disagreed in several statements within the opinion.

111   HEB Ministries at 661.

112   HEB Ministries, footnote at 667.

supported by little or no meaningful educational attainment. This would undermine the legitimate objectives of precluding issuance of fraudulent degrees and ensuring that society could rely on the attainment of a college degree as evidence of meaningful postsecondary educational accomplishment.[113]

The Texas Supreme Court would have been well advised to follow the sage counsel of the Massachusetts Supreme Court, which concluded, in a similar case regarding a secular degree that a school claimed was not a degree:

> "Degree," as used in this statute, is any academic rank recognized by colleges and universities having a reputable character as institutions of learning, or any form of expression composed in whole or in part of words recognized as indicative of academic rank, alone or in combination with other words, so that there is conveyed to the ordinary mind the idea of some collegiate, university or scholastic distinction.

> While this definition may not include all instances, it is sufficiently accurate for the present case. The ordinary diploma of public or private schools, simply certifying to the completion of a course of study, does not contravene the statute. But when a title like "Doctor," commonly associated with unusual skill acquired by academic or professional study in schools or colleges, is conferred either separately or associated with other words, the statute is violated.[114]

The Texas court concluded that the Coordinating Board had unreasonably constricted the purse of words from which the seminary could draw terms for the credentials that it issued. The seminary was left with the words "certificate" and "diploma"

---

113   HEB Ministries at 685.

114   Commonwealth v. New England College of Chiropractic, 221 Mass 190, 108 N.E. 895 (1915).

available, without words such as "master" or "doctor" attached. As Justice Jefferson noted in dissent,

> Words like "bachelor's," "master's," and "doctorate" have acquired meanings that permit them to stand on their own, even absent the noun – "degree" – they are usually understood to modify. When these absolute adjectives are used as marks of educational attainment, they represent the conferment of "degrees" …[115]

Exactly. In fact, the classification of terminology used by the Texas Coordinating Board is a very common limitation that states apply to secular schools, too, which the Texas court seems not to have known.

Oregon law, which is fairly typical, divides all educational entities that issue postsecondary credentials into two kinds, degree-granting and non-degree-granting. As of 2009 there were 128 degree-granting institutions[116] and 290 nondegree postsecondary schools[117] operating in Oregon, not counting a couple of hundred that were operating via distance education without proper authorization. The degree-granting schools use the terms associate, bachelor, master and doctor. The nondegree schools use certificate and diploma. This is normal practice in the U.S. and has nothing to do with restrictions on religious institutions.

The Texas court's conclusion that limiting the seminary to issuing credentials called certificate and diploma was an unconstitutional restriction on free exercise of religion is mistaken. It has no connection to religion and certainly is no special burden.

The terminology (e.g. a "bachelor" of something vs. a diploma certificate in the same subject) is the driver, the *basis* for distinguishing among schools. The Texas Coordinating Board

---

115 *HEB Ministries, Inc. v. Tex. Higher Educ. Coordinating Bd.*, 235 S.W.3d 627, 668 (Tex. 2007) (Jefferson, C.J., dissenting).

116 Records of the Oregon Office of Degree Authorization.

117 Or. Dept. of Education data; see http://www.ode.state.or.us/search/results/?id=83, and communication to author from Shirley Arvin, ODE, on file with author.

did not create this terminology or apply it to schools; it, like similar agencies in all other states, *responds* to it. Indeed, the words bachelor, master and doctor or their equivalent are in nearly worldwide use. Although program content varies somewhat, these terms refer to degrees and not to any other kind of educational credential (except for the modified term "baccalaureate" in certain secondary school contexts).

A school chooses the terminology it wishes to use depending on whether or not it wants to grant *degrees*. Tyndale Seminary chose terminology that by centuries-old definition can *only* be used for degrees, yet the court declared that credentials called "Doctor of Philosophy" are not degrees. This is simply a misunderstanding or willful avoidance of educational norms and terminology, which the dissenting justices, to their credit, did not buy. We expect justice to wear her blindfold, but she needs to sneak a look at objective reality.

There is some entertainment value in watching the court sail its otherwise reasonably sound legal vessel into the Nomenclature Shoals: it reaches off the chart of educational normalcy to assert, as the court did, that the terms associate, bachelor, master and doctor are not intimately, historically, uniquely and irretrievably connected with degrees – the degrees that the court implausibly insisted that the Tyndale Seminary was not issuing, and the authority for which the court declares it was not considering.

The fatal terminology shoal across which the Texas court unwisely sailed in order to get to the goal it wanted is also exposed owing to the way the court treated the two leading modern state cases. The court accepted the New Jersey court's reasoning in *Shelton College* because in that case, the school issued a wide variety of degrees, some of which were nonreligious. It rejected the Tennessee court's decision in *Clarksville School* because in that case, the seminary only issued religious degrees, which the Texas court seems to have viewed as a protected act under the First Amendment.

I say "seems" because the court then declared that in Texas, a degree is not a degree, thus its basis for rejecting the Tennessee decision is curiously decoupled from the actuality of the *HEB Ministries* case. The court avoided the issue by stating that the question of degree-granting authority was *not before the court*.[118] Apparently that question, which was raised by the Coordinating Board and was a key part of the lower court decisions, departed the building with Elvis, for that is the only way the court could have avoided it.

The basic problem that the plurality did not detect as it sailed off to its logical doom is that if degree-granting authority were not before the court, then *Shelton College* and *Clarksville School* were irrelevant and the court did not need to address them at all. Both are expressly degree-authority cases. It seems that degrees were before the court after all, when it served the inscrutable goals of the plurality.

The portion of the Texas plurality opinion that assumes that a nondegree can be called by names such as bachelor, master or doctor was wrongly decided; the dissenting justices are correct on that question.

This case was discussed in a recent opinion by the Texas Attorney General, who concluded that the decision was solely about the school's religious activity and that "*HEB Ministries* does not prohibit the board from handling a complaint involving a religious institution's *secular* program of study" (emphasis in original). This suggests that, at a minimum, any non-religious degrees issued by such a Texas school would be subject to state authorization.[119]

In fact, all degrees require state authorization and degrees issued by unauthorized colleges such as Tyndale can be treated as invalid in other states and nations. Users of these credentials have no complaint, as the Texas court said they are not degrees.

What is the net effect of the Texas split decision on the law of religious exemptions? Probably not a great deal, partly because of that court's clumsy and ineffective assertion that the seminary

---

118 "In fact, the Coordinating Board found that Tyndale awarded degrees, and HEB Ministries did not appeal that determination" Justice Jefferson, in dissent.

119 Letter opinion No. GA-0902 from Greg Abbott, Attorney General of Texas, to Raymond Paredes, Texas Commissioner of Higher Education, Dec. 22, 2011.

was not issuing degrees. It seems very unlikely that another court would go very far into that particular logical cul-de-sac.

Even if it did, the fact that the Texas court expressly *denied* that it was considering the issuance of degrees has the effect of handing future litigators a mush-ball instead of a precedent. Any argument that the *HEB Ministries* case can be used as supportive authority in a case that clearly *does* involve degree-granting comes with legal dry-rot. The opinion is, in short, a paper pussycat.[120] See the following case study for a recent federal appellate decision expressly declining to follow *HEB Ministries*.

---

120   One subsequent Texas case leans on HEB Ministries in part. *Inst. for Creation for Research Graduate Sch. v. Tex. Higher Educ. Coordinating Bd.*, 2010 U.S. Dist. LEXIS 60699 (W.D. Tex. June 18, 2010), involves questions of a denial of a certificate of authority to issue degrees to a religious institution, with the court siding with the Higher Education Coordinating Board on competing motions for summary judgment. This case, rather than HEB Ministries, was followed by the Seventh Circuit in Ill. Bible Colleges Ass'n v. Anderson, 870 F.3d 631 (7th Cir. 2017).

CASE STUDY:

Federal Appeals Court Upholds State Authority over Religious College Degrees

In a recent case originating in Illinois, the Seventh Circuit Court of Appeals added a level of federal court confirmation to the state court norm of recognizing a state's right to control the issuance of degrees by religious colleges. In *Illinois Bible Colleges v. Anderson*,[121] the appeals court agreed with the trial court and concluded that the state's method for authorizing the issuance of degrees met constitutional requirements:

> "... the plaintiffs' Free Exercise claim fails because the statutes are neutral laws of general application and apply equally to secular and religious institutions. The plaintiffs' Equal Protection claim fares no better: While the state statutes exempt older educational institutions from the governing mandates, the law is clear that, when no improper discrimination is involved, the government may include a grandfather clause in legislation without violating the guarantee of Equal Protection. Finally, the student-plaintiff alleges a violation of his right to practice a profession of his choice. But the regulations do not impact that choice. Rather, they merely determine whether he may obtain a degree from specific post-secondary institutions."

This case was brought prior to any of the plaintiff colleges actually applying for state authorization, though the colleges raised what is called a "facial" challenge; in essence saying that it would be impossible for the language to be constitutionally applied. The court left open the religious colleges' ability to raise

---

121 No. 16-1754 ILLINOIS BIBLE COLLEGES ASSOCIATION, et al., Plaintiffs-Appellants, v. LINDSAY K. H. ANDERSON, Chair of the Illinois Board of Higher Education, Defendant-Appellee. Appeal from the United States District Court for the Northern District of Illinois, Eastern Division. No. 1:15-cv-00444, Sharon Johnson Coleman, Judge. Decided August 29, 2017

specific issues of unconstitutional application of state laws should they choose to apply for state authorization and be denied for impermissible reasons. The Bible colleges asserted that they had a constitutional right to be free of improper state intrusion into their religious practice. The Court responded that without actually applying for authorization the colleges had no way to show that the state had done anything wrong.

The court also supported the traditional view that degrees are a government-backed credential by saying "It is only if the Bible Colleges seek to issue degrees that they must comply with the standards of the Illinois statute; only when the colleges venture into the secular sphere is regulatory oversight required." The opinion included several express references to the need for state oversight in ensuring quality and consumer protection.

In discussing the *HEB Ministries* case from Texas, the Seventh Circuit noted that

> "the Bible Colleges argue the Illinois statutes violate the *Lemon* test based on the plurality opinion in *HEB Ministries*, 235 S.W.3d 627, 647 (Tex. 2007). *HEB Ministries*, of course, is a Texas Supreme Court case and is not controlling. In any event, we find the analysis flawed."[122]

The way the court handled certain issues provides a mild warning to states that regulation can go too far. For example, there is an apparent conflict in Illinois law because the statute governing nondegree schools has an express exemption for nondegree religious awards, e.g. certificates. The statute governing degree-granting schools seems to define "degree" very broadly to cover any conceivable label. The court hinted that the state should not go that far, as religious training needs to be able to award some kind of certificate or diploma.

One side issue in this case may prove important over time. A student claimed that he could not practice his chosen profession because he could not get a degree from one of the affected

---

122 Ill. Bible Colleges Ass'n v. Anderson, 870 F.3d 631 (7th Cir. 2017), at 638.

schools. The court in essence said that a potential student "does not have a constitutional right to obtain a degree from a college which refuses to comply with State regulations even if that impacts his marketability." We may see this language quoted down the road.

This case is directly applicable in the states of Illinois, Indiana and Wisconsin, but because there is so little modern federal case law on this subject, the Seventh Circuit's decision becomes the de facto leading case for the country. Because the court expressly agreed with the Supreme Courts of Tennessee and New Jersey and with the dissent in the notorious HEB Ministries case in Texas, the national degree-authorization norm has received a significant additional anchor point and HEB Ministries has been effectively de-clawed.

The 'religious exempt' concept in theory and practice

There are many so-called 'religious exempt' colleges around the U.S., but in every case the exemption is expressly established or formally allowed by the state legislature. This is therefore a hybrid system under which the state in effect delegates its degree authorization powers to churches that want to issue degrees.[123] In many, but not all, cases the degrees issued by these colleges must have a religious title[124] and are designed for use in ecclesiastical settings. The analysis of their status and effect differs considerably if they issue non-religious degrees.

These "exempt" schools are mostly, but not entirely, very small church-basement operations and are overwhelmingly

---

123 An alternate view is that the law recognizes that churches have an innate right to train their leaders and this right necessarily includes degree-granting authority. This view is more difficult to support on historical grounds, as degree-granting authority was effectively a royal monopoly for so long prior to colleges coming to American shores, and once they began here. See the discussion of Harvard's early history in JOHN BRUBACHER & WILLIS RUDY, HIGHER EDUCATION IN TRANSITION: AN AMERICAN HISTORY 1636-1956 (1958), pp. 22-23.

124 Oregon had nineteen degree titles in use by religious exempt colleges as of April, 2009. Examples include Master of Divinity, Bachelor of Christian Studies and Associate of Theology.

attached to "neo-Protestant" churches. Very few have any connection to a denomination; they are highly local.

A survey conducted by the Oregon Office of Degree Authorization in 2007 asked states to indicate how many such schools they had. In the 32 states[125] that responded, there were 758 religious-exempt degree-granting institutions reported, most of which are unaccredited. Given that there were only about 4,200 accredited degree-granters in the U.S. at that time,[126] the number of religious degree-granters operating with no oversight at all is astonishing.

Religious exemption for degree-granting colleges is a controversial practice in postsecondary education. Twenty-nine states do not allow it at all, and in those states where it is established in law, it is all but universally done contrary to the wishes of higher education professionals. As Stewart and Spille pointed out in their excellent overview of the problems with religious exemptions,

> There are at least three big losers in this situation. The nation's authentic religious community is the most obvious of these: its good name is being taken in vain. Accredited higher education institutions, particularly those with ties to well-established religious bodies, are another victim: the integrity of degrees is being compromised. A third loser is the general public, as its members are exploited and "served" by persons — especially "counselors" — who hold meaningless degrees.[127]

---

125 Alaska, Arizona, Arkansas, California, Colorado, Connecticut, Florida, Georgia, Hawaii, Kansas, Kentucky, Louisiana, Michigan, Minnesota, Mississippi, Missouri, Nevada, New Hampshire, New Jersey, New Mexico, North Dakota, Ohio, Oklahoma, Oregon, Pennsylvania, South Carolina, Tennessee, Texas, Vermont, Washington, Wisconsin and Wyoming responded to the survey.

126 As listed in the HIGHER EDUCATION DIRECTORY, 2008-09 edition.

127 David Stewart & Henry Spille, *Religious Exemptions Threaten Higher Education's Integrity.* EDUCATIONAL RECORD (American Council on Education, Spring 1993, p. 46-50). This problem has not improved in the years since Stewart and Spille wrote. For an excellent and entertaining look at this subject in detail, see STEVE LEVICOFF, NAME IT AND FRAME

Twenty-one states and Puerto Rico allow religious exemptions in some form.[128] The colleges operating under these laws are operating legally under the laws of their states, therefore the degrees are probably technically valid, at least in situations where the degree-granters are named, though no one knows or can find out, in most cases, whether the academic programs issuing the degrees are any good or even exist at all. In eleven states[129] that don't require review of religious exempt applications, the providers may be simply mail-order degree mills – no one knows. In this situation, accreditation serves as a useful qualitative screen, as so few exempt schools are accredited.

In many states, religious exempt degrees can only be issued with degree titles that are clearly religious in nature.[130] This idea has usually been uncontroversial, though it has provided an undercurrent of argument in two significant cases discussed in the previous chapter.

IT (1995). *See also* JASON BAKER, BAKER'S GUIDE TO CHRISTIAN DISTANCE EDUCATION (2000), which discusses accredited religious schools that offer distance education and is more easily available (via Baker Books, Grand Rapids, MI) than Levicoff. A second edition is expected, and updated information is available at http://www.bakersguide.com/.

128 These jurisdictions exempt religious degree-granting schools from state degree authorization laws: Arizona, California, Florida, Georgia, Hawaii, Indiana, Iowa, Louisiana, Maryland, Minnesota, Missouri, New Mexico, North Carolina, Oregon, Puerto Rico, South Dakota, South Carolina, Utah, Virginia, Washington, Wisconsin. Most of these allow issuance of degrees with religious titles for "religious purposes" only. Oregon law requires religious exempt colleges to meet certain statutory standards (ORS 348.604), so is not a full exemption. Oregon does not allow any unaccredited college to issue doctorates (OAR 583-030-0025(3)), and this also applies to religious exempt schools.

129 This figure includes California 2007-2009, which then had no law allowing the establishment of any nonpublic degree-granter. Therefore religious degree-granters counld not start either.

130 Examples include Georgia, Minnesota, Missouri, Oregon, South Carolina, South Dakota, Virginia and Washington.

Is religious exemption legally possible?

We see religious exemption done, but *can* it be done, given what we know of the law of degree-granting authority? The great weight of U.S. legal opinion, and the norm in other nations, on the question of degree-granting authority is that governments control degree authorization. However, in 21 states, governments have chosen to delegate that authority to churches and religious schools. Can states do this?

There are two basic approaches to religious exemption in the U.S., with a fairly even split among the states that allow exemptions.[131] In some states, the law requires that a religious degree-granter apply for exemption and meet certain standards to become classified as an exempt college.[132] In other states, exemption is structured as a sort of veil of ignorance that the state places over its eyes and ears: religious colleges can do whatever they want to because they are religious, and the state will ignore them.[133]

I see no significant issue in the first situation. The state has chosen to place its name behind the issuance of degrees by specific degree-granters that have proven themselves to meet what standards the state requires. The fact that the standards are, in most cases, essentially nil is a policy decision that the state legislature has made. The state nonetheless has exercised its ability to *authorize a degree-granter by name*, which is a traditional authority that states have and which rests on the comfortable bulk of most court decisions. The state has chosen to become the guarantor of the validity of degrees issued by those specific colleges.

This is bad education policy, and such degrees, if unaccredited, should always be treated as nonstandard and never

---

131 For types of state laws conferring religious exemption on degree-granting colleges, see Appendix.

132 The law in Colorado, Florida, Georgia, New Mexico, Oregon, Virginia and Washington requires an application and formal state determination of eligibility for exemption. Some Oregon providers were grandfathered.

133 The law in Arizona, Hawaii, Louisiana, Minnesota, Missouri, South Carolina, South Dakota and Wisconsin requires nothing in the way of application or proof of status.

accepted for secular employment, but I see no reason why a state whose legislature lacks commitment to academic standards can't do it.

It is much more difficult to find support for the "see no college, hear no college" approach of states that simply ignore any religious degree-granters. The same consistent cluster of cases that supports the state's right to authorize degree-granters makes very clear that such authorization must be done *expressly* and must be on a *college-by-college* basis.[134]

There is no basis in U.S. case law (other than the dubious Texas decision noted above, which the court expressly denied was about degree-granting authority) for the position that a college can acquire degree-granting authority without formal written governmental authorization. I do not see how classifying a category of unknown educational entities as exempt from state requirements can constitute authorization for the issuance of degrees. Authorization to exist as educational institutions, yes, but not authorization to issue degrees.[135]

The practical problem with the hands-off approach by states can be seen very clearly in the LaSalle case in Louisiana, in which the state, having declared religious colleges exempt, attempted to require that LaSalle prove it was a tax-exempt entity, and lost the case.[136] The fact that the owners of LaSalle eventually went to prison on federal mail-fraud charges for selling degrees did not undo the state appellate court decision.

To say that an unknown, unknowable, constantly changing universe of degree-granting institutions, none of which are even

---

134   See Chapters 1 and 2 for a detailed discussion of these cases. The leading cases are Nat'l Assn. of Certified Public Accountants v. United States, 53 App. D.C. 391, 292 F. 668 (1923), *cert den.* Oct. 6, 1923 and Townshend v. Gray, 62 Vt. 373, 19 A. 635 (1890).

135   My discussions of the basis of degree-granting authority with one of the country's higher education law experts raised the issue of whether the Tenth Amendment by itself provides sufficient authority to a state that wants to allow any entity to issue college degrees without express state authorization. My colleague thinks that this may be a valid approach. I disagree. Available case law, of which there is a moderate amount, all supports the idea that degree authorization must be express and in writing. But the Tenth Amendment is a land of mystery.

136   See Ieyoub v. World Christian Church, *supra.*

known by name, let alone *authorized* by name to issue degrees by the state that is nonetheless responsible for the validity of the degrees that they issue, is not a defensible legal or academic structure. This is especially true, perhaps fatally so, when the degrees can be in any subject[137] or can be used in any job. In that situation, the state's police power to protect the public trumps practices that are asserted to be of a religious nature,[138] but which occur in a paddock traditionally limited to the state's herds.

Some exemption laws imply that the degrees issued are to be used for a religious purpose.[139] There are obvious enforcement issues with such an approach, because once a degree is issued, it can travel anywhere and be used for many purposes, often with the tacit support of employers or clients. This can be viewed as a victimless crime in the sense that if all involved parties agree that a meaningless credential[140] meets the needs of a given situation, no harm is done. Such situations are relatively rare, since many religious degrees, as noted by Stewart & Spille, *supra,* are used in positions related to counseling, where third-party

---

137 Georgia, Louisiana, Oregon, Minnesota, Missouri, South Carolina, South Dakota, Virginia and Washington require exempt schools to use only religious degree titles. Arizona, Colorado, Hawaii and Wisconsin do not specify that religious exempt degrees must have religious titles.

138 See the *Smith* cases in Note 105.

139 For example, New Mexico's exemption law reads, in pertinent part:
5.100.2.8   INSTITUTIONS OR ORGANIZATIONS EXEMPT FROM THE ACT:
A. The Post-Secondary Educational Institution Act specifies several bases for exemption from provisions of the act. An institution, organization, or other entity wishing to qualify for exemption from the act must present to the department the information necessary for the department to determine eligibility for exemption. Upon determination of eligibility by the department, the following may be granted an exemption:
... (3) a nonprofit institution whose sole purpose is to train students in religious disciplines to prepare them to assume a vocational objective relating primarily to religion; ... .

140 I say "meaningless" because it is generally impossible for an external observer or client to determine whether degree programs at exempt colleges are genuine. Some are; some are not, and people who want to tell the difference cannot ask the state, which in all other cases would have records of the school's programs, complaints and the like.

clients, and potentially their families, employees, employers and clients, are affected and are subject to harm by unqualified professionals.

One question that remains undiscussed in case law is whether a church, if it is effectively delegated the authority to authorize the issuance of degrees in a "see no college" state, becomes a state actor, given that only governments can authorize the issuance of degrees. This is a rather large discussion beyond the scope of this chapter, but would create an unusual entanglement likely to fail the *Lemon* test, which disallows excessive government entanglement with religion.[141]

An argument soundly based in the history of higher education as well as the First Amendment can be made that religious institutions have great freedom to train people who will assume positions of leadership in sponsoring churches. To that extent I see no problem allowing religious organizations to issue credentials to their pastorate and other church officials. This is not the state's concern.

However, *degree-granting* authority is not inherent in churches. Degrees are by definition government-backed credentials, and the authority to confer them is in the sole gift of governments. That has been true for hundreds of years and was true when the United States was founded.

If a degree is a public credential, then it should be treated as such. If degraded degrees issued by exempt schools could realistically be limited to use in sectarian roles within the churches that produced them, the problem might be somewhat contained (the social cost of degrading those churches being within the acceptable limits of church-state separation), but degrees are extremely portable and their origins often unchecked.

It is necessary that the state retain and regain authority over degrees issued by religious organizations. If a church opens a restaurant, it is not exempt from health inspections. If a priest starts pulling teeth, is he not practicing dentistry? Degrees are a public credential of value. It is necessary that all religious exemptions, if they need to exist at all, be carefully constructed to

---

141   Lemon v. Kurtzman, 403 U.S. 602 (1971).

limit degrees to those with religious titles and to limit their issuance to schools that meet certain basic standards.

CASE STUDY

Tracking a religious credit worm from origin to destination

A small, startup unaccredited religious college naturally wants to build its credibility, serve its students and become an established institution. It therefore starts doing exciting things:

- Enters into a consortium agreement whereby it is under the aegis of a regionally-accredited college that accept its credits despite the fact that the regionally-accredited college has accreditation standards saying that it should not accept credits from unaccredited suppliers.

- The regionally-accredited provider also fails to notice that the new college has not yet received state authorization or exemption allowing it to issue college credits at all. The accreditor, of course, does not know this either.

- The startup then makes an arrangement with an unauthorized, unaccredited provider in another state to offer a portion of the program online, without either state or the regionally-accredited partner knowing.

- Many of the faculty teaching for both the startup and its online partner do not have degrees in the fields they are teaching, or their degrees are from unaccredited providers.

What is the proper action for the two state regulatory agencies and the accreditor to take? Should the new provider be approved by the state? Should it be exempted, if that is allowed under state law? Should the accreditor act to limit the use of credits that have traveled a roundabout path through two unaccredited providers? Which state is responsible for overseeing the academic quality of the program? Which entity is responsible for handling complaints about the program?

Problems with Oregon's exemption law and how other states can avoid them

Oregon's hybrid religious exemption statute is coupled to a statute governing discriminatory action by employers.[142] This provision was inserted in order to placate conservative legislators who wanted to ensure that degrees issued by exempt, unaccredited Portland Bible College were broadly usable in Oregon even though the state never evaluated the school.[143]

The net result of this 2005 legislation is that unless an Oregon employer is very careful in how any degree qualification

---

142 ORS 659A.318, which reads:

659A.318 Discrimination relating to academic degree in theology or religious occupations prohibited.

(1) If an employer requires an applicant or employee to have an academic degree from a post-secondary institution to qualify for a position, but does not require a degree with a specific title, it is an unlawful employment practice for the employer to refuse to hire or promote or in any manner discriminate or retaliate against the applicant or employee only because the applicant or employee meets the educational requirements for the position by having a degree with a title in theology or religious occupations from a school that, when the degree was issued, was a school described in ORS 348.594 (2)(d) on the date preceding July 15, 2005, or was a school exempt from ORS 348.594 to 348.615 under ORS 348.604.

(2) If an employer other than a public body, as defined in ORS 192.410, offers employees benefits of tuition reimbursement, educational debt reduction, educational incentive or educational contribution or gift match for educational services provided by a post-secondary institution and the employer does not restrict the program to specific institutions or degrees with specific titles, it is an unlawful employment practice for the employer to refuse to offer the benefit to or in any manner discriminate or retaliate against an employee because the employee attends or seeks to attend a school that is:

(a) A school that was, on the date before July 15, 2005, described in ORS 348.594 (2)(d); or

(b) Exempt from ORS 348.594 to 348.615 under ORS 348.604. [2001 c.621 §93; 2005 c.546 §11]

143 Portland Bible College was grandfathered in the legislation (546 OR. LAWS 2005), so that it never had to go through the initial state review. At that time, one of its major supporters was House Speaker Karen Minnis (R-Gresham), who, with her husband former State Senator John Minnis, attend the church that operates the college.

requirements are stated in advertising and job descriptions, it may be required to accept a degree issued by an unaccredited degree-granter whose program quality is completely unknown and unknowable. It also requires employers who underwrite college costs for employees to treat exempt schools the same as standard schools, while providing no method through which an employer can determine whether the exempt school has a legitimate academic program—or any at all.

This is a very poor approach to both law and policy. Forcing employers to accept pieces of paper that may be worthless serves no legitimate public policy goal and places public health and safety at risk.

Exemption from state degree-granting standards should extend only to items of a religious nature. That category includes the content of a religious college's curriculum and to those aspects of its operation that relate to its religious nature, such as student conduct codes and expectations of faith on the part of students and faculty.

Exemption should not include many other aspects of college operation. There is no meaningful religious aspect to such things as proper award of credit based on actual student work (versus giving it away for no work), appropriate fee refund policies, access to a library and similar requirements. Issues such as faculty academic qualifications fall in an area of overlapping interests. The state has an interest in ensuring that faculty hold degrees appropriate for teaching their subjects. For example, someone with no background in mathematics should not be teaching it at the college level. Religious authorities have a legitimate interest in ensuring that faculty are able to teach subjects with religious content in a manner appropriate to the faith.

States that have religious exemptions in their postsecondary oversight structures need to examine those exemptions carefully to make sure that they only do what is necessary to ensure a proper relationship between state interests and religious interests. Such laws should not allow churches to issue degrees with no state oversight, nor should they compel employers to treat exempt degrees about which nothing can be known the same way as state-authorized or accredited degrees.

PART B – Special Situations and Issues

Chapter 4

International Degrees used in the United States

Alan L. Contreras

There is considerable discussion these days about the portability of higher education credentials. This often includes the idea that degrees and other credentials should be usable across international boundaries with a minimum of evaluative action. The underlying goal is a good one—to make it easier for academics to work in their field across borders. In practice, this requires at least some minimal care.

Evaluation Methods

If all degrees truly were created equal, there would be no need for any kind of evaluation of their content, as we would know in advance that it was essentially the same. Unfortunately that is not the case in the real world, so we need some kinds of evaluation in order to decide what a degree really is.

Most countries maintain lists of their own legitimate degree-granting institutions. There are exceptions, and there are situations in which such lists are not very useful owing to corruption, incapacity and failure to keep current. For example, the governments of several small island states will happily give you a list of the colleges they have authorized. Unfortunately these countries don't have any real universities and the list is made up of degree mills.

The problem of inaccurate lists exists in some larger countries as well, mainly in western and central Africa and south Asia, but it can potentially crop up anywhere owing to local corruption or simple errors.

For these reasons, as well as because of questions about the details of a particular degree, international evaluation of college degrees has become a specialized profession and in any situation in which a degree is in doubt, such professionals should be used. The principal providers of such services in the U.S. are the American Association of Collegiate Registrars and Admissions Officers (AACRAO)[144] and the twenty or so organizations that are members of the National Association of Credential Evaluation Services (NACES).[145] There are a few other providers of such services that are reputable—ask around—but there are also some remarkably well-constructed fakes that provide this service for the degree mills that own them.

Apostilles

Anyone who works in higher education credential evaluation will quickly encounter what are called "apostilles," sometimes more formally Apostilles of The Hague, after the 1961 conference that developed the concept. These documents are intended to make it easier to determine whether a document, e.g. a license, issued in one country is genuine and therefore potentially recognizable in another country. Sometimes they are attached to a degree in order to assert the validity of the degree.

Unfortunately, apostilles don't tell us anything about the nature of the entity that has provided someone with a piece of paper called a degree. The apostille action is closer to that of what a notary does in the United States. For this reason, an apostille tells us little more than that a person owns that piece of paper. The convention at the Hague that developed this system did not expressly list college degrees as one of the items to be "certified" by apostille, and in fact these international add-ons should not be used for that purpose, beyond determining that the person standing in front of you holding the document is probably the same person who obtained the apostille.

Degree mills of the seediest kind routinely use apostilles as a way to make their products look good. Unfortunately this

---

144 http://www.aacrao.org/key-topics/international-admissions-credential
145 Naces.org

practice has become so common that the whole concept of the apostille has been tainted for use by genuine colleges.

Authorization by bogus nations

The world of international credentialing contains a few very unusual players. These include such quasi-countries as the Hutt River Province in Australia, the Principality of Seborga in Italy and others. Degree mills will sometimes flag their products in these places and assert that this counts as national authorization for the issuance of degrees. It doesn't.

Effect of U.S. Accreditation on the Validity of Foreign Degrees

U.S. accrediting associations are private entities and they can accredit any institution that their own rules permit. Whether that has any effect on how a given entity treats the foreign school depends on the purpose for which the accreditation "flag" is used. There are certain issues to keep in mind.

First, U.S. accrediting associations are "federally recognized" only for purposes of collegiate eligibility for Title IV aid and a few other federal programs, e.g. programs for veterans. This means, among other things, that a voluntary accreditation of a foreign provider by a U.S. accrediting body conveys no "federal recognition" useful for the foreign entity. The relationship is among two private entities (unless the foreign provider happens to be public). For this reason, benefits applicable inside the U.S. to an entity accredited by a *federally recognized* accrediting association do not automatically accrue to a foreign provider.

CASE STUDY

Michigan law and the *Almeda* case

In *City of Fraser v. Almeda Univ.*, 2016 Mich. App. LEXIS 82 (Mich. Ct. App. Jan. 14, 2016) the Michigan Court of Appeals concluded that Michigan law regarding the "issue" of degrees in the state applied to the entity that does business under the name Almeda University even though that business sells degrees from the nation of St. Kitts and Nevis in the Caribbean and only ships them to Michigan.

The court concluded that acceptance of payment from a Michigan buyer and subsequence mailing of the documents to the buyer in Michigan is enough to establish the state's jurisdiction. Of note is that Almeda admitted in this case that its degrees were fraudulent under the meaning of Michigan law.

Chapter 5

STATE AUTHORIZATION AND PROFESSIONAL LICENSURE

The Intersection of the Federal Government, State Authorization Agencies and Professional Licensing Boards

Sharyl J. Thompson

Introduction

There have been many changes in the world of state authorization since the last edition of this book. The State Authorization Reciprocity Agreement (SARA) has been adopted in 49 of the 50 states, California being the one state that is not a member. As of January 31, 2020, membership in SARA has decreased the concentration on individual state authorizations for the 2,058 institutions that have been approved to operate under SARA. Only institutions in California or those institutions that choose not to participate in SARA (and those that have physical campuses outside their home state) must seek authorization on a state-by-state basis.

However, an issue that has risen in visibility and compliance is programs that may lead to a professional license or certification – academic requirements for a person who desires to work in a licensed field. SARA does not cover the professional licensure requirements, so institutions must be aware of the ways and by whom professional licensure programs are regulated.

National and state professional licensing boards have academic and other standards that individuals must meet in order to practice in a licensed field. These standards are not new, but institutions are becoming more aware of the effect they have on their faculty and their students, especially when they enroll students from out-of-state.

As complicated and nuanced as state authorization is, professional licensure standards can be even more difficult to understand and navigate. Higher education institutions often don't have the resources nor do they want to take on the responsibility of knowing state professional licensing regulations and standards. It takes a lot of hard, detailed work – the results of which can change quickly and with little or no notice from a state professional licensing board.

Adding to the complexity of professional licensure requirements, the U.S. Department of Education has new regulations going into effect on July 1, 2020 that increase the oversight of professional licensure programs for institutions approved to use federal financial aid (Title IV) funds for their students. (https://www.govinfo.gov/content/pkg/FR-2019-11-01/pdf/2019-23129.pdf). The new regulations expand oversight to include professional licensure programs offered through *campus-based programs* as well as online programs. The regulations clearly place the onus on the institutions to know whether their professional licensure-track programs meet the academic requirements for a professional license in the state in which the student is "located." Gaining this knowledge requires state-by-state research of the professional licensure academic requirements followed by a comparison with the institution's program(s). Once an institution has purchased or completed the necessary research and determined if the professional licensure or certification requirements in each state where a student is "located" are met, it then needs to publicly disclose that information to prospective and current students.

Background

State authorization is a formal determination by a higher education agency (commonly a higher education board or commission) that allows an institution to conduct certain activities within its borders. Examples of these activities (often called "triggers") include online students located in a state, face-to-face recruiting, targeted advertising, internships or other supervised field experiences, employing a faculty member who resides in a particular state, or having a branch campus in another state. Institutions not participating in SARA are responsible to know the triggers in each state and U.S. territory, and either not conduct the activity that triggers the need for authorization, or apply for and obtain state authorization, which gives permission to conduct activities in the state. Every state is different. Triggers vary from state-to-state. The cost and time to obtain authorization also varies widely.

For the purposes of this chapter, "state authorization" is the general term used for what some states call registration, certification, accreditation, license to operate, etc. Some states authorize the institution as a whole while others, like Arkansas, North Carolina, and Ohio authorize on a program-by-program basis. State authorization is *not* the same as program approval by a state professional licensing board.

As stated earlier, each state professional licensing board has varying standards for occupations that require a professional license or certification. Examples include P-12 teacher, school administrator, school counselor, school psychologist, mental health counselor, family therapist, social worker, psychologist, nurse, physical therapist, CPA, etc. The national or state professional licensing boards have standards an academic program (the institution) must meet in order for a graduate to be eligible for a license. They also have requirements an individual graduate must meet to be eligible for a license, such as criminal record, age, legal residence, etc.

When distance education first broke on the horizon, neither state authorization regulators nor professional licensing boards were prepared for the issues it would uncover. Historically, institutions' graduates earned their degrees on a campus located in one state and the institutions needed only to be concerned about graduates' eligibility for a professional license in that state. At that time, the state authorization entities were seldom, if ever, in contact with the professional licensing boards, and the professional licensing boards often didn't know there was a state authorization entity in its own state. Distance education changed that.

Because distance education allows a student taking courses while located in one state to earn a degree from an institution located in another state, the state authorization entities are concerned that professional licensure-track programs meet professional licensure requirements in their state. Professional licensing boards may require an institution to have state authorization before they will review and determine if the program(s) meets their professional licensing requirements. Some state authorization entities require out-of-state institutions to bring their licensure-track programs before their professional licensing boards before granting authorization.

Why is this important? The answer is consumer protection. It is not uncommon for students to enroll in a licensure-track program with little or no understanding about whether they will be eligible to get licensed once they have completed the program. Until recently, institutions could leave it up to the student to make that determination. Now the onus is placed on the institution with disclosure requirements. Disclosure requirements are codified at the federal and state levels. SARA also has professional licensure disclosure requirements that are designed to 'track' with federal rules.

Lawsuits have been filed against institutions because their graduates (in another state) thought they would be eligible for a professional license in their home state, only to find out that wasn't the case. So, these graduates spent thousands of dollars and often years of time and effort (which cannot be redeemed) to earn a degree, only to find out the degree did not meet the standards for them to be eligible for a professional license in the state where they intended to practice. The state authorization entities, SARA and the federal government see this as a matter of consumer protection, believing individuals should know in advance whether taking a program from any institution meets the standards and regulations necessary for professional licensing eligibility.

Professional Licensing Boards

Listed earlier were examples of occupations for which a professional license or certification is required. States typically have many different professional licensing boards and some boards issue more than one classification of license. For example, the counseling board in a state may issue licenses for a licensed professional counselor, a licensed clinical professional counselor, an addictions counselor, or even a school counselor. A person can search the Internet for "professional licensing boards in" and name a specific state. From there, links will lead to specific information.

Institutions sometimes mistakenly believe the eligibility of professional licensure is automatic where there is a national exam or a national programmatic accrediting body and the state-specific requirements don't apply, so no research is necessary. However, states may, and often do, have additional state-specific requirements that institutions need to meet.

Institutions are frequently expanding campus-based programs to an online delivery system or adding new online course or program offerings that may not lead to a license, endorsement, or certification in the state where the institution is located, but those same programs may lead (or students may expect to them lead) to a professional license or certification in another state. For example, an institution may decide to offer a graduate program in reading and literacy without intending it to lead to a license or endorsement – and it may not in the state where the institution is located. However, another state may have a reading and/or literacy endorsement available for teachers with which graduates may get a pay increase. The institution offering these programs need to be aware of these differences so it can clearly disclose where a program does or does not lead to a professional license or endorsement.

It is not uncommon for a state authorization regulatory agency to require an out-of-state institution offering online programs leading to a professional license or certification to also have those programs approved by that state's professional licensing board(s). Some states even require post-licensure nursing programs to go before the state's Board of Nursing for approval – but some boards of nursing do not approve post-licensure programs. If program approval is required and a student graduates from a program that does not have the necessary approval, that graduate may not be able to obtain a professional license in the state in which they are located. In some states, program approval by the professional licensing board must be obtained prior to the institution receiving state authorization; in other states, state authorization must be obtained first and professional licensing board approval second.

Institutions sometimes mistakenly believe the eligibility of professional licensure is automatic where there is a national exam or a national programmatic accrediting body and the state-specific requirements don't apply, so no research is necessary. However, states may, and often do, have additional state-specific requirements that institutions need to meet. That is why state-by-state research is still critically important.

State Reciprocity: SARA and its Professional Licensure Program Limits

The State Authorization Reciprocity Agreements (SARA) have advanced quickly and unified national policies have been established by the National Council for SARA. As of the time of updating this chapter, forty-nine states, the District of Columbia and several U.S. territories have become members of SARA. This voluntary agreement between states and U.S. territories allows an institution authorized in its home state to be authorized in all other states that are members of the agreement. SARA has been a huge step forward in reducing costs and duplication of efforts for institutions while still protecting students from fraudulent practices.

However, as advantageous as SARA is, it does not cover the requirement (in some states) for institutions to have licensure-track program approval by state professional licensing boards. Nor does the state authorization reciprocity afforded by SARA cover the individual states' professional licensing regulations and requirements or reciprocity of professional licenses between states. The same professional license in one state may have different requirements in another state, such as the degree required, the number of internship or practicum hours, the qualifications of supervisors and faculty, and if programmatic accreditation is mandatory. All institutions offering licensure-track-programs, including those institutions that participate in SARA, need to research these requirements on a state-by-state, license-by-license basis so the proper disclosures can be published.

SARA has requirements regarding disclosures about professional licensure-track programs. Knowing the requirements cannot be left up to the current or prospective students. Each professional licensing board in every state is autonomous and establishes and governs the standards a program or a graduate must meet in order to receive a license or certification in a professional field. So, while SARA provides reciprocity for state authorization for academic programs, it does not provide reciprocity or automatic approval for licensure-track programs by professional licensing boards.

There is some good news, however. The National Council of State Boards of Nursing (NCSBN) has formed an agreement between states for guidelines for prelicensure distance education nursing programs, which has similarities to SARA (https://www.ncsbn.org/7451.htm). Under this agreement, the nursing licensure board in the institution's "home" state approves the distance education nursing program. The home state ensures there will be faculty supervision over clinical students in other states. While the agreement has been approved, states have been asked to make the required changes to implement this approval format by 2020.

In addition, the National Council of State Boards of Nursing (NCSBN) has formed a Nurse Licensure Compact (NLC) allowing graduates of pre-licensure, undergraduate programs to obtain an LPN/VN or RN license in multiple states. This provides the opportunity for nurses to practice in their home state and all other NLC states (https://www.ncsbn.org/34.htm). As of the date of this chapter revision, there are thirty-two states that have implemented the NLC.

Another compact with professional licensing boards is the National Association of State Directors of Teacher Education and Certification (NASDTEC) (http://www.nasdtec.net). This compact is more widely known, but often misunderstood. This agreement is a collection of over 50 individual agreements by states and Canadian provinces. Although it is very helpful for individuals in licensed educator professions, it does not provide for an automatic two-way acceptance between the member states and provinces. There is no guarantee that if State A accepts teaching certificates from State B that State B will accept certificates from State A. Also, there is no guarantee that if someone is a fully licensed teacher in one state that he or she will be fully licensed in another. There may be additional professional licensure requirements like coursework, assessments, state-specific testing, or classroom experience before receiving a full license in another state. The NASDTEC website provides details.

How do these licensure compacts affect institutions with pre-licensure nursing or educator programs and state authorization? A state authorization entity may accept documentation showing licensure reciprocity as evidence that residents of their state are eligible for a license upon graduation. However, if there are additional licensure academic requirements, the institution should show the state authorization entity how it will equip its students to meet those requirements and how it will disclose that information to its current and prospective students.

A Look to the Future

Since 2010, the U.S. Department of Education has worked toward setting regulations governing distance education. After negotiated rule making when the committee could not come to a consensus on what the regulations should say, the U.S. Department of Education proposed another set of regulations in 2016. The proposed regulations were open for public comment, after which the Department decided what the final regulations would include. Although it was expected these regulations would be published prior to November 1, 2016 so they could go into effect on July 1, 2017, they weren't published until late December, making them effective July 1, 2018. These regulations were very onerous for institutions, and non-compliance put institutions' ability to disburse Title IV federal financial aid at risk. Portions of those regulations were set aside due to a lawsuit regarding due process.

Most recently, new, less onerous regulations were proposed, vetted through the Negotiated Rule Making process where consensus was reached, and later published by the Department of Education with an effective date of July 1, 2020 (see chapter 34 CFR Parts 600, 602, 603, 654, 668, and 674). One significant change is that disclosures for professional licensure-track programs *will include campus-based programs as well as online programs.*

The new regulations may be found at:

https://s3.amazonaws.com/public-inspection.federalregister.gov/2019-23129.pdf.

With another presidential election coming in 2020, the future of federal regulations for higher education is unknown. In the meantime, institutions outside of California and approved to participate in SARA need to be familiar with the SARA Manual, posted on the NC-SARA website. Institutions in California or those in other states that choose to not participate in SARA need to abide by the state authorization regulations in all 50 states, the District of Columbia and the U.S. territories. All institutions offering professional licensure-track programs need to be aware of licensure and programmatic requirements across the country and publish the required disclosures.

Important considerations for institutions

State authorization coupled with professional licensure is very complicated. Below are a few items for institutions to consider.

1. Professional licensing board requirements and standards are not covered by SARA. Institutions participating in

SARA must still deal with individual state professional licensing boards.

2. Institutions need to know the professional licensure requirements in states outside their home state and publish appropriate disclosures. This includes the programmatic or academic requirements (number of credits, internship or practicum hours, accreditation, coursework requirements, etc.), needed for licensure.

3. Institutions may be required to have their professional licensure-track programs approved by a licensing board in another state in order for their graduates in that state to be eligible for a license.

4. Some state professional licensing boards will forego an individual program review if the program has programmatic accreditation. For example, some states will accept (or require) that a psychology program leading to a professional license be accredited by the American Psychological Association (APA). For educators it may be CAEP accreditation; counselors, CACREP accreditation, etc.

5. Some state professional licensing boards do not review programs from out-of-state institutions. If that is the case in a state where the state authorization agency requires such program approval as a condition for authorization, the institution will need to communicate with both state entities to find a workable solution.

6. Disclosures regarding professional licensure apply to both online and campus-based programs.

7. An institution needs to determine the ways to comply and how often it will disclose professional licensure information to its students and prospective students. SARA and some state authorization entities require such notification and the federal government already requires

this through the misrepresentation and gainful employment rules currently in effect along with the new federal state authorization regulations going into effect July 1, 2020, and ties compliance with these rules to the institution's Title IV eligibility.

8. Like state authorization regulations, professional licensing board regulations and standards change so a periodic review by the institutions is wise. Institutions need to allocate resources for keeping abreast of the changes and build action plans for review and compliance into their regulatory compliance efforts.

Resources for professional licensure

There is no one source to go to for information on professional licensure. There are websites that provide information on professional licensure, with varying degrees of accuracy. For example, there is a website where individuals wanting to become a licensed marriage and family therapist can look up their state's requirements (http://www.mft-license.com). The Association of Social Work Boards (ASWB) has a website with useful information for individuals and institutions (https://www.aswb.org/public) regarding the social work profession. An Internet search can lead to other website resources as well. As mentioned earlier, the NASDTEC website is a good resource for finding the contact information for each state educator licensing board and it provides information on the reciprocity of educator licenses. Although sites like these are helpful, one should always confirm the academic requirements by reading the professional licensing board's standards and requirements themselves.

Conclusion

This has been an overview of the cross-section between state authorization and professional licensure. There are many details and nuances involved for compliance with the multiple regulations and standards.

Although state authorization and professional licensure is complicated, compliance is doable for institutions as long as they are willing to provide the human and financial resources necessary. The most important point is – don't ignore state authorization and don't ignore what needs to be done pertaining to licensure-track programs offered across state lines.

Chapter 6

Federal Action through early 2020

Russell Poulin
Cheryl Dowd

A brief history of the state authorization regulation

The concept behind the Department of Education's state authorization regulations for distance education is very simple. Students receive millions of dollars in federal financial aid. Just as an institution is expected to follow the laws of the state in which it is headquartered, it should be expected to follow the laws of all other states in which it is disbursing federal financial aid.

What starts off as simple can often get very complicated. This is especially true when factoring in the many and varied regulations of the fifty states, misconceptions, misinformation, a lawsuit, institutional leadership dodging responsibility to follow the laws, and others trying to hijack the regulation for their own purposes. To those not paying close attention, the whole issue quickly appears exceptionally byzantine.

Before exploring the federal regulations introduced over the last few years, it is important to remember some basic facts:

- States have jurisdiction over education within their boundaries.
- State authorization regulations are based upon the state's interest in protecting its consumers of education.
- The federal government has influence in only a few areas. Among those are federal financial aid and treating students equitably. The federal government cannot tell states directly what to do about education, but they can use funding (such as financial aid) to influence state actions.

- The states vary wildly in their oversight of distance education. Some states require very little of out-of-state institutions, while a few have rules that appear to be inspired more by a sense of protectionism than consumer protection.

- Although widely believed, it is a myth that states are making money off of state authorization regulations. Maybe a few states are, but, even with these funds, many states are underfunded to perform basic consumer protection tasks.

- Authorization laws enacted by the states preceded the federal regulation and will continue whether or not there is a federal state authorization regulation.

The October Surprise of 2010

For a regulation to go into effect on July 1 of any year, the final version of that regulation must be published in the Federal register by the end of October of the preceding year. On October 29, 2010, final regulations covering the "Program Integrity[146]" of federal financial aid programs were released by the U.S. Department of Education. These regulations were the result of a long process to codify the intentions of the 2008 Higher Education Opportunity Act. This was the latest in a string of "reauthorizations" by Congress of the original Higher Education Act of 1965. The reauthorizations of the Act contain the requirements that institutions must meet to be eligible to disburse federal financial aid.

The October 2010 regulations contained a surprise. Questions arose during the comment period when the regulations were proposed about how distance education fits into federal expectation. In response to those questions, a new paragraph was added that had not been included in the version circulated for comment:

---

146 Program Integrity Questions and Answers - State Authorization: https://www2.ed.gov/policy/highered/reg/hearulemaking/2009/sa.html

(c) If an institution is offering postsecondary education through distance or correspondence education to students in a State in which it is not physically located or in which it is otherwise subject to State jurisdiction as determined by the State, the institution must meet any State requirements for it to be legally offering postsecondary distance or correspondence education in that State. An institution must be able to document to the Secretary the State's approval upon request.

After calls for clarification to Fred Sellers of the U.S. Department of Education staff, WCET (the WICHE Cooperative for Educational Technologies) issued a blog post on the regulation, held a room-filling, pop-up session at the WCET Annual Meeting, and hosted Sellers on a webcast in January. The higher education community was surprised at the federal requirement and experienced a large dose of denial.

Expanding on the 75 words listed above, the main tenets of those explanations were:

- Effective July 1, 2012, the Department of Education would begin checking to see if an institution was in compliance with the rules of any state in which it disbursed aid to a student enrolled via distance education.
- Any institution that issued aid in a state in which it was not in compliance with state laws could be asked to refund any financial aid disbursed to those students.
- In a separate regulation, institutions also had to inform students of the state's complaint process in the state in which the student is located.

2011: Uncovering Problems with Implementation of the Regulation as Planned

Over the 2010-11 holiday season, WCET, SREB (Southern Regional Educational Board), and the University of Wyoming partnered to study the regulations of all 50 states and published the results. As a result of this research and other conversations with institutional personnel, we learned:

- Regulations regarding whether an institution needed to be authorized in a state varied greatly from state to state. Some states required extensive documentation in prescribed formats while others required no action at all. In 2011, the State Higher Education Executive Officers (SHEEO) organization assumed the responsibility of maintaining a survey of state regulations[147].

- Most states used many criteria to determine "physical presence" in a state, which would trigger the need for institutional approval. Owning a building or holding face-to-face session between faculty and students in a state are obvious signs of an institution's "physical presence." There were other, less obvious activities that could "trigger" the need for approval. Examples include: direct marketing, requiring students to go to a location for testing, having an employee in a state (including adjunct faculty), conducting field or practical experiences, and having a server in a state.

- Only about a dozen states required any approval if the only activity in a state was enrolling distance education students. Even so, colleges and universities would often find that some unit of their institution was conducting one of the activities that triggered the need for authorization in another state.

- State regulatory offices were not consulted about the regulation and they were not ready for the forth-coming avalanche of inquiries and applications.

- Regulatory information was often hard to find and was not always clear to understand.

- If an institution read the federal regulation on the day it was released and applied to all fifty states on the very next day, they would not be able to meet the July 1, 2011 effective date. Some state processes take so long (sometimes a year or more) that there simply was not enough time to become authorized. This was especially

---

147   State Higher Education Executive Officer's survey of state regulations: http://sheeo.org/projects/state-authorization-postsecondary-education

true if hundreds of institutions would be applying at the same time.

Additionally, in talking to colleagues offering distance education, the following facts emerged:

- Almost no public or private, non-profit institution was in compliance outside of its home state.
- Most for-profit institutions were in compliance in every state in which they enrolled students.

These assumptions were later confirmed in a series of surveys conducted by UPCEA and WCET[148].

2011-2012: Clarifications through 'Dear Colleague' Letters

WCET notified Sellers of its findings and he confirmed them in conversations with others in higher education leadership. Over the next couple years, the Department released a series of official letters (commonly called 'Dear Colleague' letters) that added detail to the regulation and delayed enforcement of it. Some of the most notable highlights included:

- Moving the enforcement date back to July 1, 2014 and creating a series of "good faith" indicators that institutions could use to demonstrate progress toward obtaining compliance in the states necessary to cover their students.
- The list of state complaint processes could be compiled and maintained by a third-party entity, but the institution was still responsible for assuring its accuracy.

---

148 "What are Institutions Doing (or Not Doing) About State Authorization" Survey:
http://wcet.wiche.edu/initiatives/research/upcea-wcet-sa-survey

These clarifications were responsive to the reality in the field and were well-received by most higher education professionals. Equally, many in higher education leadership did not like this new rule. They hoped it would go away. Many of them remained in denial that states still expected them to follow their laws whether or not there was a federal regulation on the books.

2011-2012: The Lawsuit Vacating the Distance Education Regulation

The Career College Association[149] (an organization primarily composed of for-profit institutions) filed a lawsuit against the Department of Education challenging several of the Program Integrity regulations released in October 2010. State authorization was among the items they targeted in that suit, in which they expressed two main objections:

1. The Department did not have the jurisdiction to issue such a regulation.
2. The Department did not follow the proper notification procedures in issuing the regulation.

The lawsuit was heard by the United States District Court for the District of Columbia. The Court found that the Department failed to comply with the Administrative Procedure Act's[150] (APA) notice requirements prior to issuing the distance education regulation in 2010. As a result, the distance education language (34 CFR 600.9 (c)) was "vacated" on the grounds that the Department did not distribute any language related to distance education as part of the public comment period. The vacating order meant that the Department could not enforce the distance education part of the regulation.

---

149 During the lawsuit, they changed their name toe the Association of Private Sector Colleges and Universities (APSCU). The organization has subsequently change its name to Career Education Colleges and Universities (CECU).

150 Administrative Procedure Act: https://en.wikipedia.org/wiki/Administrative_Procedure_Act_(United _States)

The Career College Association appealed the case to the United States Court of Appeals for the District of Columbia Circuit. The Appellate Court subsequently ruled[151] to affirm the decision of the District court to vacate 34 CFR 600.9 (c) for failure to provide the required notice. The Court remanded to the District Court with instructions to remand the challenged regulations to the Department for reconsideration. On the main objections raised in the original lawsuit, the Appeals Court ruled that:

1. The Department *did* have the authority to issue such a regulation. Since the Department was responsible for overseeing the process of issuing federal financial aid, it could place whatever requirements it wished on institutions disbursing that aid.
2. The Department *did not* follow the proper notification procedures. When the Department issued its proposed regulation in 2010, there was no specific language regarding distance education. The Department agreed that it had not previously specifically addressed distance education, but said that the final language was a "logical outgrowth" of questions it received about the proposed regulation. The Appellate judges disagreed with the "logical outgrowth" argument and affirmed the ruling to vacate the regulation. Remanding the regulation back to the Department meant that they could not enforce it, but they could go back and correct the technical errors they committed in not using the proper notification process.

As a result, the Department issued a "Dear Colleague" letter on July 27, 2012[152] stating they would not enforce the distance education regulation. They reminded institutions that they

151 "Court Deals Second Blow to Federal State Authorization Regulation," WCET *Frontiers*:
https://wcetfrontiers.org/2012/06/05/state-authorization-appeal/
152 "USDoE Will Not Enforce Its Distance Ed State Authorization Regs, But Questions Remain," WCET Frontiers:
https://wcetfrontiers.org/2012/07/30/usdoe-will-not-enforce/

"continue to be responsible for complying with all State Laws as they relate to distance education[153]." At that time, it was unclear when, or if, the Department would attempt to revive this rule.

2012: Reciprocity Became a Viable Option for State Compliance

Even prior to the federal regulation being released, Excelsior College headed a project funded by a Lumina Foundation planning grant to determine a common set of standards to be used for state authorization. A reciprocal agreement among states would allow one state to recognize the authorization of an institution by another state. Among the benefits of a reciprocity agreement:

- Student Protection. Only about a dozen states were regulating institutions that were "distance-only," meaning that the institution conducted no other regulated activity in the state other than enrolling students in distance courses. Therefore, students in the great majority of states were unprotected by complaint processes or laws in the state in which they were located.

- State Oversight. State authorization offices have been historically underfunded. A thinly-staffed regulatory agency is better suited to oversee the few institutions within its own state as opposed to watching hundreds of institutions spread across the country.

- Institutional Applications. The widely-varied state compliance processes for out-of-state activities was deemed very difficult and expensive for institutions to manage.

A drafting team created recommendations and versions of a national program of reciprocity for interstate compliance of distance education. A $2.3 million grant from Lumina

---

153 Dear Colleague Letter ID: GEN-12-13, U.S. Department of Education: https://ifap.ed.gov/dpcletters/GEN1213.html

Foundation was awarded to implement the agreement. The final draft of the State Authorization Reciprocity Agreement (SARA) was released in January 2013. Indiana was the first state to join SARA in February 2014. As of February 2017, forty-seven (47) states plus the District of Columbia have joined SARA. More than 1,500 institutions are operating under SARA. This also meant that any federal regulation would need to address this emerging method of obtaining approval in a state.

2013-2014: The Department Reconsiders Regulations

On November 20, 2013, The U.S. Department of Education announced its intention to form a negotiated rule making committee to address a set of federal financial aid issues, including the state authorization of distance education. A negotiated rulemaking committee is tasked with preparing proposed regulations to address the issues assigned to the committee. The committee must reach consensus on all issues for the regulations to be released as proposed regulations for public comment. In this case, "consensus" means that all committee members must vote in the affirmative on all issues placed before the committee. If consensus is not reached, the Department is free to determine its own language to be released as proposed regulations to the public for comment.

The Federal Register, Vol 78, No 224[154], indicated that the Program Integrity and Improvement Committee would address the following varied topics:

- Cash Management of funds provided under the title IV Federal Student Aid programs, including the use of debit cards and the handling of title IV credit balances.
- State authorization for programs offered through distance education or correspondence education.
- State authorization for foreign location of institutions located in a State.

---

154 U.S. Department of Education, "Program Integrity Questions and Answers – State Authorization":
https://www2.ed.gov/policy/highered/reg/hearulemaking/2009/sa.html

- Clock to credit hour conversion.
- The definition of "adverse credit" for borrowers in the Federal Direct PLUS Loan Program.
- The application of the repeat coursework provisions to graduate and undergraduate programs.

Applications were sought from individuals representing a wide range of interests by institution type, state-level attorneys general, and consumer protection groups. Russell Poulin, one of the co-authors of this chapter, was selected to represent the distance education community and Marshall Hill, Executive Director of the National Council for SARA (NC-SARA, the program's general oversight board) was seated as an alternate. Given the wide range of issues addressed and interest groups represented, there were several members who had great depth on some issues and little knowledge about others. The Department of Education also was seated as a voting member of the committee.

Prior to the first meeting, the Department released new proposed language on each issue. Many Committee members were surprised when the original 75 words of the language were expanded to several pages and multiple subsections. The Department insisted on a provision that would have been a back-door way to force states to conduct an "active review" of every out-of-state institution offering distance education in the state. Because the Department cannot directly regulate states, this was a "back-door" effort as the requirements would be on the institution to assure that the states in which they served students had such a review process. This would result in institutions lobbying legislatures in other states to change their laws.

Additionally, after several attempts, the Department was unable to define "active review." A similar problem had already arisen on the state authorization rules that the Department had promulgated for the oversight of in-state institutions. Due to a similar lack of definition, states were struggling with meeting that requirement. Many on the Committee did not wish to repeat that scenario.

There were also attempts to implement additional consumer protection measures and to expand some notifications to cover non-distance students. In the end, the "active review" issue was the key barrier to institutional representatives agreeing to the proposed regulation. Of the sixteen Committee members, only five supported the final proposed state authorization regulation. The Cash Management regulation also did not reach consensus.

After the failure to reach consensus, the Department was free to draft its own language for proposed regulations for public comment. Despite the good work of the Committee and the desire of the Department to release new state authorization regulations, in June 2014, Ted Mitchell (Under Secretary for Postsecondary Education), announced a 'pause'[155] on state authorization to give the Department time to "get it right." In July 2015, Ted Mitchell made comments to a meeting of the National Association of College and University Attorneys that made it sound as if a new regulation was not coming any time soon.

2016: More Surprises! New Regulations Released

Reminiscent of the October surprise of 2010, the Department, with only 6 months left to go in the administration, provided a mid-summer surprise with a July release of new proposed federal regulations for state authorization of distance education.[156] The new proposed regulations appeared to address some of the concerns of the 2014 Negotiated Rulemaking Committee, such as the opportunity for states to regulate activities in their state as they choose rather than a federal requirement to create an "active review." Additionally, the regulations provided specific requirements for public and individualized notifications and disclosures for institutions offering activities for distance or correspondence students. Questions arose about the definition of consumer protection which became a topic of concern for clarification by the

---

155 "U.S. Department of Education Pausing on State Authorization," WCET *Frontiers*: https://wcetfrontiers.org/2014/06/26/pause-on-state-auth/

156 "Department of Education State Authorization for Distance Education Regulations-A First Look," WCET *Frontiers*: https://wcetfrontiers.org/2016/07/22/department-of-education-state-authorization-for-distance-ed-regulations-a-first-look/

Department. The regulations were open for comment for a short period over the summer.

October 31, 2016, came and went with no new federal regulations for state authorization of distance education. That date was the deadline for formal action to be taken for the new regulation to take effect on July 1, 2017. The national election of 2016 brought about a change in administration and a change of philosophy for federal oversight of higher education. Despite these changes, the holiday surprise of 2016 occurred on December 19, 2016, when the Department released the Program Integrity and Improvement regulations for State Authorization of Postsecondary Distance Education, Foreign Locations.[157] The effective date for this rule was set for July 1, 2018.

Of greatest concern in the new regulation was a provision regarding reciprocity agreements. Based on comments from some state attorneys general, the Department changed the language so a *"State authorization reciprocity agreement does not prohibit any State from enforcing its own statutes and regulations, whether general or specifically directed at all or a subgroup of educational institutions."* This seemed to be a death knell for reciprocity as it would be untenable for each state to enforce its own set of rules: there would be no reciprocity.

In a call and subsequent conversations with one of the co-authors of this chapter, leaders in the Department of Education said that was not their intent. A last-minute letter from Department Under Secretary Ted Mitchell[158] confirmed an interpretation that was more friendly to reciprocity agreements: *"In other words, a distance education reciprocity agreement may require a State to meet the requirements and terms of that agreement in order for the State to participate in that agreement."* While this letter did not have the force of law, it was a clear statement of the Department's intent in supporting reciprocity.

---

157 "A Lump of Coal for SARA and Other goodies in the State Authorization Regulations," WCET *Frontiers*:
https://wcetfrontiers.org/2016/12/16/a-lump-of-coal-for-sara-and-other-goodies-in-the-state-authorization-regulations/

158 "Education Department Confirms 'Reciprocity' Definition Clarification," WCET *Frontiers*:
https://wcetfrontiers.org/2017/01/19/ed-confirms-reciprocity-definition/

2017: What the New Administration Wrought

After rumblings that it might do so, the new administration did not avail itself of the Congressional Review Act (CRA), which allows Congress to overturn regulations released in a recent time period. While other regulations enacted at the end of President Obama's term were repealed, the Congress and the administration did not remove the new final Federal State Authorization Regulations (aimed at distance education) that had been released in December 2016. However, in February 24, 2017, President Trump signed Executive Order 13777, "Enforcing the Regulatory Reform Agenda," which established a Federal policy "to alleviate unnecessary regulatory burdens."

The Executive Order directed that Federal agencies establish a task force to evaluate existing regulations and make recommendations to repeal, replace, or modify regulations. To that end, the Department of Education sought input with a request for written public comment during Summer 2017 as well as the opportunity to participate in one of two public hearings in the Fall 2017. The purpose of which was to give the public the opportunity to identify any education regulations that should be candidates to repeal, replace, or modify.

2018 – Came in Like a Lamb but Went Out Like a Lion

The new year began perhaps too quietly. There was no response provided from the Department of Education about the outcome of the written public comments or public hearings from the previous summer and fall. State Authorization regulations were still on the calendar to become effective July 1, 2018, despite many requests for clarification and guidance from key stakeholders.

In May 25, 2018, the Federal Register, Vol. 83, No. 102 reported that the Secretary of Education proposed to delay, until July 1, 2020, the effective date of the regulations proposed by the Obama administration. The proposed delay cited concerns raised by regulated parties. The announcement in the Federal Register asserted that there needed to be adequate time to conduct negotiated rulemaking to review and possibly revise the regulations. This announcement was part of an accelerated rulemaking process to create a "delay rule" for these regulations to delay the effective date. A fifteen-day public comment period (relatively short for such postings) for the proposed delay was offered. The announcement noted that "a longer comment period would not allow sufficient time for the Department to review and respond to comments and publish a final rule."

On July 3, 2018, the Federal Register, Vol. 83, No. 128 reported that the Secretary of Education delayed until July 1, 2020, the effective date of selected provisions of the 2016 final regulations in order to provide adequate time for negotiated rulemaking to review and possibly revise the regulations. The selected provisions included 34 CFR 600.2 – Definitions: state authorization reciprocity agreement; 34 CFR 600.9(c) – State Authorization of distance education; 34 CFR 668.50 – Institutional disclosures for distance or correspondence programs. Only 34 CFR 600.9(d), state authorization of additional locations or branch campus located in a foreign country, was not delayed and therefore became effective on July 1, 2018.

The announcement of the delay cited two letters received by the Department that were influential in their decision to delay the effective date of these regulations. The letters were reported to have been received in February 2018. The first letter was from the American Council on Education (ACE) stating that students from certain states may be ineligible for federal financial aid as some states, including California, did not currently have a complaint process for all out-of-state institutions.

The second letter was from the WICHE Cooperative for Educational Technologies (WCET), National Council for State Authorization Reciprocity Agreements (NC-SARA), and the Distance Education Accrediting Commission (DEAC). This letter described the widespread concern and confusion about implementation of the 2016 final regulations due to complaint process issues as ACE described, state authorization compliance based upon the term "residence" which would be in conflict with state regulatory compliance and needed clarification about the implementation of required disclosures. The Department indicated that mere guidance would not be satisfactory to address the concerns raised.

On July 31, 2018, the Federal Register, Vol. 83, No. 147 provided the announcement for the Department of Education's intention to establish a negotiated rulemaking committee. The announcement provided the format for which the Department wished to proceed including the use of subcommittees. The Department proposed to address a long list of varied topics related to accreditation, state authorization, distance education, innovation, and eligibility of faith-based entities among others.

Three public hearings and opportunity for public comment were provided. Despite widespread concern regarding the number of topics and the unprecedented plan to use subcommittees, the Department of Education closed 2018 by moving forward choosing main committee members plus members for three subcommittees from nominations that had been submitted to the Department of Education representing regulated parties.

Meanwhile, in August 2018, the National Education Association (NEA), California Teachers Association (CTA) et al. filed an action against the Department of Education and Secretary DeVos in the United States District Court in the Northern District of California. The basis of the lawsuit is centered on the Department's alleged failure to follow proper process to develop and issue the Delay/Rescission Rule under the Administrative Procedure Act (APA) which governs the process for federal agencies to develop and issue regulations.

This failure to follow APA process allegedly resulted in injury to the plaintiffs who due to the delay were not able to avail themselves of disclosures to make informed decisions about their education. The Plaintiffs sought a court decision to vacate the Delay Rule and cause the 2016 final regulations to become effective. The case then proceeded through months that followed.

2019 – Action Packed! Negotiated Rulemaking; Consensus; Court Ruling; Proposed Regulations, Final Regulations

The 2019 Federal Negotiated Rulemaking for Accreditation and Innovation met January 14, 2019 – April 3, 2019. The issues were identified and split among three subcommittees: Distance Learning and Educational Innovation Subcommittee, Accreditation and Innovation Subcommittee, and TEACH Grants Subcommittee. The main committee and subcommittees met each month. All of the subcommittee hearings and main committee hearings were available for streaming online for the public. The subcommittees served to provide research and advise the main committee on the wide range of issues. The main committee had the responsibility of developing the regulations and reaching "consensus," which is defined as 100% agreement by all negotiators on all proposed language, in order for the regulations to move forward.

The Department of Education typically begins the committee meeting with the opportunity for the negotiators to brainstorm to develop language for regulations. Given the unusually long list of issues, the Department initiated the rulemaking process with suggested language for the negotiators to consider. Notable in the initial language was the proposal to completely elimination the state authorization for distance education regulations. The negotiators argued that those regulations should be preserved as institutions disbursing federal financial aid should be expected to follow state laws, and the Department personnel agreed.

In addition to an unprecedented use of subcommittees and providing suggested regulatory language, the rulemaking process also used an unprecedented voting method of voting in what the Department of Education described as "buckets" of issues. The similarly situated issues were then voted upon by the main committee and ultimately reached consensus by voting unanimously in favor of the regulations in each bucket on April 3, 2019. Consensus having been reached, that language then becomes the proposed regulations to be released for public comment. After consensus was reached, the Department indicated that it was likely that the consensus language would be released in multiple packages of proposed regulations.

On April 26, 2019, the judge for the United States District Court in the Northern District of California found for the plaintiff in NEA and CTA et al. v. DeVos and Department of Education et al. The ruling indicates that the Department of Education did not have just cause for a shortened negotiated rulemaking process of only a 15-day public comment period to develop and implement the Delay rule for the 2016 Federal State Authorization Regulations.

The court cited multiple public comments and representation at public hearings from WCET and the WCET/State Authorization Network (SAN). These public communications indicated that the Department of Education had notice of the implementation concerns and ambiguities for which clarification was requested prior to the February 2018 letters cited in the Department's reasoning for the delay rule. The Delay rule was vacated by the court. The judge chose to delay the ruling for 30 days to allow the Department to prepare direction for regulation implementation. Therefore, the 2016 Federal regulations became effective on May 26, 2019.

On June 12, 2019, in the Federal Register, Vol. 84, No. 113, the Department of Education announced the first package of proposed regulation that came from the consensus language of negotiated rulemaking. The first package included the regulations for accreditation and state authorization for distance education that came from consensus. A thirty-day period for public comment was provided. The proposed regulations for state authorization for distance education include the following outcomes:

- A reaffirmation that Federal financial aid is tied to an institution being able to demonstrate that it has the approval of the state (either directly or through a reciprocity agreement) to serve students in that state.
- The proposed "reciprocity" definition continued to include the ambiguous language about applicability of individual

"general" or "direct" state laws that could conflict with reciprocity policy for which the state agreed to follow.

- Regulatory language change to focus on student location rather than residence to determine the jurisdiction where institutions had to demonstrate they had obtained state approval.
- Distance education disclosures are eliminated due to duplication with similar requirements elsewhere in the Code of Federal Regulations.
- Professional Licensure disclosures that had not previously been part of the Code of Federal Regulation was added and applies to all modalities.
- Eliminated the requirement to "document" a state's complaint process since some states did not have a complaint process.

While most people in higher education focused on the outcomes of the negotiated rulemaking that were recently released, less attention was initially paid to the outcome of the Court ruling on the case brought by the NEA and others. On July 22, 2019, the Department of Education formally acknowledged that the Court had set a May 26, 2019 effective date of the 2016 Federal Regulations for State Authorization for distance education. This announcement appeared in the Federal Register on July 29, 2019, Vol, 84, No. 145.

Although consensus was reached from negotiated rulemaking and proposed regulations on state authorization had been released, no new Federal Regulations were in effect to replace the then-effective 2016 Federal Regulations for State Authorization that had become effective due to the U.S. District Court ruling vacating the "Delay Rule."

Guidance for compliance with the regulations, in the form of a Q & A document, was also provided by the Department. This is the first guidance that was provided by the Department of Education related to the 2016 Federal Regulations. While much broader guidance had been requested in the letters cited by the Department in its request to delay the rules back in 2018, the new guidance narrowly focused on the documentation of a state complaint process as required by 34 CFR 600.9(c)(2). The question addressed the applicability of the regulation if the State in question lacks its own complaint process or does not participate in a state authorization reciprocity agreement. The Department indicated that the institution must comply with this documentation requirement in order to be Title IV-eligible.

This issue has conversationally been referred to as the "California Problem" due to the lack of compliant process and oversight of public or private non-private out-of-state institutions that offer distance education to students in California. Unofficial estimates at the time indicated that as many as 80,000 students taking distance courses from out-of-state institutions could have had their financial aid eligibility at risk.

California officials responded quickly with a complaint process plan. The Department of Education reviewed the new California process and (although it did not fully meet the Federal requirements) considered it acceptable dating back to May 26, 2019. Their guidance on the matter stated that the Department still expected that California will make modifications to address "compliance challenges." With those actions, the aid eligibility for the students in question was preserved.

The Federal Register published the Department of Education announcement of Final Federal Regulations on State Authorization and Accreditation on November 1, 2019, Vol. 84, No. 212. Section 482 (c) of the Higher Education Act (HEA) requires that regulations affecting programs under Title IV must be published in final form by November 1 prior to the July 1 start to the next award year. Therefore, the effective date of these final regulations is July 1, 2020.

However, the Secretary of the Department of Education may exercise authority provided by the HEA to designate specific regulations for early implementation at the discretion of the regulated agencies. Secretary DeVos chose to identify the following state authorization regulations: 600.2; 600.9; 668.43; and 668.50 to be subject to early implementation beginning November 1, 2019, at the discretion of each institution. These 2019 State Authorization Federal Regulations replace the 2016 State Authorization Federal Regulations.

One will recall that when consensus is reached by negotiated rulemaking, the language, subject to review of grammar and conflict of law, must then be what becomes the proposed regulations that are subject to public comment. Public comment offers the opportunity to request language clarification from the Department to make edits to language so that it can be implemented by the regulated community.

The language for the proposed regulations for State Authorization and Accreditation came from the consensus language. However, the Department expressed that many public comments expressed opposing views in requesting clarification of the language of 600.2 that defined "state authorization reciprocity agreement." The final regulations modified the definition of state authorization reciprocity agreement from the proposed language to direct that an agreement cannot prohibit a state from enforcing its own general-purpose State laws and regulations outside of State authorization of distance education.

This revision clarifies the specific applicability of state laws enforceable against an institution when the institution participates in reciprocity in a state participating in reciprocity. Examples include laws and regulations applicable to any business, such as for registration with the State Secretary of State or any State Department of Labor requirements.

While many support and appreciated this clarification as one that allows for consistent oversight through reciprocity, there are some groups in opposition to this change who want the state to enforce laws regardless of its participation in a reciprocity agreement. Such a rule would undermine the functionality of reciprocity.

Professional Licensure: the Compliance Challenge That May Take Years to Implement

The regulations require disclosures as to whether an institution's program meets the academic requirements for licensing in the student's location. Although professional licensure disclosures are important to allow students to make informed decisions about programs to prepare them to pursue their chosen professional career, implementing beneficial disclosures is a challenge. Efficient implementation of a disclosure process at the institution requires a thorough review of the institution's programs leading to professional licensure and research of the requirements for licensure or certification in each state for each program offered by the institution.

The notion of institutional transparency about an institution's curriculum meeting state educational requirements in other states for programs leading to professional licensure or certification is not new. Transparency and disclosures have been required for many years by State laws and regulations and also through Federal Regulations regarding misrepresentation, 34 CFR 668.72. The SARA Manual, Section 5.2, also requires institutional transparency by requiring that SARA participating institutions provide disclosures to enrolled and prospective students for courses or programs under SARA Policy about meeting educational requirements where the student is located.

The 2019 Federal Regulations require professional licensure disclosures for all modalities; face to face and distance education. A key concern for implementation is obtaining the information from the professional licensure boards in order to compare the institution's curriculum and the state educational requirements. The research required tends to cause one to recall the state by state higher education agency research that was part of the pursuit of institution approval prior to reciprocity.

While some jump to the idea that there should be some type of professional program reciprocity, they underestimate the difficulty of creating such agreements for each and every profession. It should be noted that the function of professional licenses is to protect the public by providing verification that a person has sufficient education and skills to perform the duties of the specific profession. The professional boards have an important role to protect the public not just the student. If program reciprocity is to occur, it will come from the individual professions developing that structure.

Alternatively, some place the responsibility for determining whether a program meets state requirements on the student. That expectation places a tremendous burden on students who cannot be expected to understand whether a curriculum meets state rules in a profession for which they have not taken the first class. Meanwhile, to provide full support for students, an institution must develop a thorough institutional plan to audit and assess all programs leading to professional licensure or certification offered by the institution.

Chapter 7

Interstate Reciprocity and SARA

State authorization in the context of higher education usually means one of two things. It can mean:

1. the original authority to issue degrees in the state where the provider began, or it can mean

2. the subsequent authority to operate in a state other than the original state.

SARA was brought into being to deal with subsequent authority and it uses original authority as part of its structural base.

Original authority is discussed in detail earlier in this book. Modern discussions of state authorization refer mostly to subsequent authority as applied to institutions that already have original authority to issue degrees. This situation arises most often in situations in which an institution wants to offer courses, degrees or specialized activities in a state other than the one where it began life. This is important because original authorization is valid only in its original jurisdiction. Thus a Missouri university, public or private, does not have the inherent legal authority to operate in Iowa, and vice-versa.

What this means is that establishing a branch campus, a collective download site where students gather, a field placement site for interns or various other cross-border actions by colleges potentially require some sort of authorization from the receiving state. This situation is where the term 'state authorization' is most often used. Institutions that want to operate interstate often have to pay significant fees to receiving states, go through long and complex application processes and provide significant amounts of data to other states.

Interstate Agreements and SARA

Interstate compacts or agreements are a common practice; SARA is often called "a national solution that isn't a federal solution." A standard example is the compact that allows an Idaho driver's license to be valid in every other state. Some states have special agreements, either state-to-state or brokered through a regional partner organization like WICHE, through which a state with no law school like Alaska, no library school like Oregon or no dentistry school like Kansas can 'trade' access to such programs either for a fee or in matching access, so that students can enroll and, in some cases, pay in-state tuition.

Interstate agreements such as SARA are more broad-spectrum. SARA covers only certain kinds of distance education, not physical campuses or similar sites, but it covers any programs that a college chooses to offer through distance-ed. In joining SARA, states agree that certain regulatory standards that would normally be applied to a school will be held in abeyance, with SARA policies and procedures used instead.

A Brief History of SARA

The State Authorization Reciprocity Agreements (SARA) provide a streamlined, reciprocity-based process for participating postsecondary institutions to gain approval to offer interstate distance education to students in SARA member states without individually applying to each state for such approval, subject to certain limitations. SARA centralizes the authorization process for each SARA-participating institution in a single state that SARA calls the institution's "Home State." Institutions approved by their Home States to participate in SARA must be appropriately accredited and meet academic and financial requirements designed to protect and benefit students.

The four State Authorization Reciprocity Agreements were developed from 2011 through 2013. SARA began operating in January 2014 as a nationally-standardized network with a single set of standards developed by the central office (the National Council for SARA) in cooperation with the four regions.

The original regional SARA agreements developed by the four U.S. regional education compacts differed slightly from one another and were eventually superseded by the Unified State Authorization Reciprocity Agreement ("Unified Agreement") in December 2015. The Unified Agreement is the foundational document for the SARA initiative, establishing SARA as a nationwide endeavor. It provides a rationale for reciprocity as the basis for addressing state authorization of distance education challenges and outlines the general roles and responsibilities of the various partners involved in the work of SARA.

> The current SARA Manual can be obtained online at:
>
> https://nc-sara.org/resources/guides

To implement the Unified Agreement, NC-SARA and the regional compacts continued to develop NC-SARA's Policies and Standards, eventually compiled into the SARA Manual, which specifies in greater detail the procedures, policy details, and guidance to institutions, regional compacts, and states required for the operation of SARA. The Manual is now the controlling document for SARA operational policy, superseding the founding agreements by action of the National Council for SARA in 2019.

A key feature of SARA is its voluntary nature: States may join SARA if they wish to do so and are approved for membership in SARA by their regional compact. Likewise, if a state joins, its eligible institutions have the option of participating, but are not required to do so. As of April, 2020, 49 states (all but California), the District of Columbia, Puerto Rico and the U.S. Virgin Islands are members of SARA. More than 2,000 institutions participate.[159]

How SARA Works

SARA does not cover all aspects of interstate postsecondary activity. To participate, an institution must be a U.S. based

---

159 Portions of this material are adapted from the *SARA Manual*, Edition 20.1

accredited degree-granter, meet certain financial and educational standards and agree to basic data reporting for SARA, including reporting certain kinds of complaints.

SARA allows institutions to offer distance education into any member state without going through that state's usual regulatory process. Instead, institutions go through an application process in which certain basic attributes are determined and certain standards are accepted.

Some related activities are covered by SARA. Participating institutions are allowed to place students in clinicals, internships and similar off-campus professional activities, whether or not the field placement is connected to a distance education program. There is also limited coverage for short courses (the kind normally done on a weekend or in some similar period of time) and for field trips involving a single night in another state. Longer events such as summer field sites, extended periods at museums and the like are not covered by SARA.

SARA also does not cover the rules of professional licensing boards with regard to the validity of professional licensure across state lines. This question arises most often in the case of nursing, teaching and some of the social service professions. In some cases, passing a national exam is mistakenly thought to 'automatically' create reciprocity, when in fact state licensing boards may have other requirements.

SARA does not have any effect on transferability of credits.

State Authorization Resources

SAN

The WCET State Authorization Network (SAN) is the premier organization for training and support of institutions navigating regulatory compliance for institutions' out-of-state activities. Since 2011, SAN has provided members with opportunities to participate in webinars, beginner and advanced workshops, monthly virtual meetings, discussion forums, and twice yearly face-to-face meetings. Additionally, SAN provides access to original and collected research materials as well as access to experts in the field. SAN currently assists more than 600 institutions covering all states and types of institutions.

For further information contact Cheryl Dowd, WCET/SAN Director at cdowd@wiche.edu

See also the WCET/SAN website:

https://wcetSAN.wiche.edu

SARA

SARA is the national agreement among states and regional compacts that allows participating institutions to offer distance education programs across state lines more easily. For information about SARA, see the web site at:

https://nc-sara.org

SARA can be contacted at:

3005 Center Green Drive, Suite 130
Boulder Colorado 80301

303.848.3764

SARA also maintains a list of state higher education agencies at:

https://nc-sara.org/guide/agency-list

SHEEO

The State Higher Education Executive Officers works on statewide and national policy issues affecting higher education, with a focus on public providers.

https://sheeo.org

About the Authors

Alan L. Contreras is a higher education consultant who works for SARA. He was administrator of the Oregon Office of Degree Authorization for twelve years and also worked for the University of Oregon, Oregon Community College Association and Missouri Coordinating Board for Higher Education. A graduate of the University of Oregon and its law school, he has published frequently on higher education issues in the *Chronicle of Higher Education, Inside Higher Education, International Higher Education,* and other venues. He recently published *The Mind on Edge: an Introduction to John Jay Chapman's Philosophy of Higher Education.*

Sharyl J. Thompson is a consultant on state authorization, licensing board issues and related subjects. She has gained expertise in higher education regulatory affairs and compliance for over a decade. She is an independent consultant assisting institutions with all phases of state authorization and regulatory compliance, professional licensing requirements, research, and accreditation activities including initial strategic planning, training, presenting, and completion of applications.

Russ Poulin leads WCET, the WICHE Cooperative for Educational Technologies, which focuses on the practice, policy, and advocacy of technology-enhanced learning in higher education. WCET's members hail from all fifty states and a few from Canada. As WICHE vice president, he advises on policy and projects for the regional higher education compact. Poulin represented the distance education community on federal negotiated rulemaking committees and subcommittees. He has received recognition from the Presidents' Forum, Excelsior College, and the National University Technology Network for his contributions to policies for technology-enhanced postsecondary education. Poulin received a bachelor's degree from the University of Colorado Denver and a masters from the University of Northern Colorado.

Cheryl Dowd is the Director of the State Authorization Network (SAN) for WCET. Dowd directs the activities and research for institutions and other related organizations to understand and manage regulatory compliance requirements for the out-of-state activities of the institutions. Webinars, beginner and advanced workshops, monthly virtual meetings, discussion forums, twice yearly face to face meetings, as well as original and collected research are made available to the SAN members.

118

Made in the USA
Coppell, TX
19 July 2020